STUDY GUIDES
English
Year
5
LES RAY AND GILL BUDGELL

D0189062

Contents

Content grid

 = Assess your understanding

Links to Primary Framework for Literacy Year 5

	Unit title	Focus text	Strand	Strand objective	Chat challenge
1	Unstressed vowels	List of words featuring unstressed vowels	6 Word structure and spelling	Spell words containing unstressed vowels	Check understanding of terminology, purpose and links to spelling
2	Transforming words – prefixes	Examples of prefixes: -ad, -re, -al, -im, -il, -un		Know and use less common prefixes and suffixes	Check understanding of terminology, explore derivation and links to spelling and meaning
3	Transforming words – suffixes	Examples of suffixes: -er, -est, -ion, -ism, -en, -ise, -ify			
4	Spelling patterns in plurals	Examples of plural words with exceptions		Group and classify words according to their spelling patterns and meaning	Check understanding of terminology and explore links with spelling
5	Grouping words according to meaning	Examples of auto-, circ-, bi-, tele-, -graph, micro-, de-			Explore derivation and links to spelling
6	 What have we learned?				
7	Making notes to explain things	The Earth in ancient times	7 Understanding and interpreting texts

(8 Engaging with and responding to texts) | Making notes | Check understanding of purpose and various techniques |
8	Writers' perspectives	The Runner by Keith Gray		Infer writers' perspectives from what is written and from what is implied	Explore the meaning through discussion of visualisation, prediction and empathy (Strand 8)
9	Structure of narrative texts – beginnings	Buried Alive by Jacqueline Wilson		Compare different types of narrative and information texts and identify how they are structured	Use as a basis to discuss reading habits and preferences and to plan personal reading goals (Strand 8)
10	Structure of narrative texts – story structure	Dennis the Menace, Beano			Use as a basis to compare how a common theme is presented in poetry, prose and other media (Strand 8)
11	Structure of narrative texts – endings	'How Comes That Blood?' A ballad, Anon			
12	News reports	Fred's ruler destroyed as it topples from table			Discuss purpose, audience and features
13	Instructions	Chocolate Biscuits			

	Unit title	Focus text	Strand	Strand objective	Chat challenge
14	Non-chronological reports	London	7 Understanding and interpreting texts *(8 Engaging with and respondong to text)*	Compare different types of narrative and information texts and identify how they are structured	Discuss purpose, audience and features
15	Letters	Formal letter			
16	Language for comic effect	Jokes and riddles		Explore how writers use language for comic and dramatic effects	Discuss what makes a good joke and the impact of meaning and sound
17	🚦 What have we learned?				
18	Edit and improve your work	*Little Wolf's Haunted Hall for Small Horrors* by Ian Whybrow	9 Creating and shaping texts	Reflect independently and critically on their own writing and edit and improve it	Discuss the importance of mistakes and what purpose they serve
19	Adapt non-narrative forms and styles	Caring for a kitten: Turning instruction into a poem		Adapt non-narrative forms and styles to write fiction or factual texts, including poems	Discuss the differences and similarities between text types and genres. Look at layout
20	Viewpoint through the use of direct speech	*Annie's Game* by Narinder Dhami		Vary the pace and develop viewpoint through the use of direct and reported speech, portrayal of action and selection of detail	Check on understanding of terminology and explore 'speech' together
21	Viewpoint through the use of action	*Antimorphs I, The Invasion* by K A Applegate			Check on understanding of terminology and explore 'action' together
22	Viewpoint through the use of detail	*The Otterbury Incident* by C Day Lewis			Check on understanding of terminology. Adjective and adverb
23	🚦 What have we learned?				
24	Paragraphs and order	Information text: Money	10 Text structure and organisation	Experiment with the order of sections and paragraphs to achieve different effects	Check on understanding of terminology, usage, purpose and effect
25	Changing the order of sentences	Information text: Surnames		Change the order of material within a paragraph, moving the topic sentence	
26	Speech marks	*The Adventures of Tom Sawyer* by Mark Twain	11 Sentence structure and punctuation	Punctuate sentences accurately, including using speech marks and apostrophes	
27	Apostrophes	King Arthur			
28	🚦 What have we learned?				

1 Unstressed vowels

Look carefully at these words and the help given about how to spell them.

poisonous

separate

extraordinary

conference

stationery

definitely

secretary

interested

business

Wednesday

Chat challenge

What is a vowel?

What is a consonant?

Do we pronounce vowels in all the words we use?

Are we just being lazy by not pronouncing vowels in words?

Try saying some of the words above, pronouncing every vowel – what is the result?

What spelling problems can be caused because we do not pronounce vowels in certain words?

Comprehension

1) Identify all the vowels in the words on the opposite page.

2) Pronounce all the words by breaking them into syllables.

   e.g. **sep – ar – ate, ex – tra – ord – in – ary**

3) Which three words have the most syllables?

4) What do you notice is in every syllable?

5) What does it mean when you stress a part of a word?

6) Why do you think people do not stress all the vowels when they say them?

Objective focus

1) Write out these words with the correct vowels.

   an_m_l, dict_on_ry, gen_r_lly, l_br_ry, m_rv_llo_s

2) Write the correct versions of the following words.

   discription, diffrance, genrous, intrest, misrable

3) Here are some definitions of words. Write the words correctly.

   a. Not the same: di_____

   b. Place where things are made: f_____y

   c. You have lost hope: de_____e

   d. You are sure about something: de_____e

   e. Place where you go if you are ill: ho_____

4) Write the words from question 3, breaking them into syllables. Circle the vowels in

Links to writing

1) Use ten of the words with unstressed vowels in this unit in sentences to show that you know what they mean.

2) What tricks do you know which would help someone spell these words correctly?
   jewellery, primary, lottery

3) Make a dictionary of all the words with unstressed vowels in this unit. Put them in alphabetical order with their meanings. Use a computer to do this.

2 Transforming words – prefixes

Prefixes go at the beginning of a word to change its meaning.

Prefixes can tell you what words mean.

ad- means **towards**, e.g. advance
　　　　　　　　　　　　　addition

re- means **again**, e.g. return
　　　　　　　　　　　　reanimate

al- means **all**, e.g. almighty, almost

You can make a word mean its opposite (make it negative).

mature – immature

practical – impractical　　　　　　　literate – illiterate

legal – illegal　　　　　　　　　　believable – unbelievable

happy – unhappy

Chat challenge

What is a prefix?

How is it different from a suffix?

If you make a word mean its opposite, what happens to the spelling of the word?

Can you think of any other examples?

Many prefixes come from other languages than English. What countries would these be?

Do you know any tricks for learning to spell words where prefixes have been added?

Comprehension

1) Identify the prefixes in the words on the opposite page.

2) Identify the 'roots' of the words from the examples opposite.

3) Which roots are whole words? Which words are just parts of words?

4) When you add a prefix to the root of a word to make it negative (make it an opposite), does the spelling of the root change?

5) Use a dictionary to find ten more examples using these prefixes to transform words.

Objective focus

1) Give the opposites of these words, adding the prefixes *in-* , *dis-* or *un-* where possible.

a. accurate	**d.** common	**g.** agree	**j.** continue
b. happy	**e.** sufficient	**h.** belief	**k.** attentive
c. able	**f.** necessary	**i.** allow	**l.** own

2) Which of the following words are not correct? Give the correct spelling.

a. inpossible

c. nonimaginable

b. already

d. uninspiring

3) Write these words using the correct prefixes.

a. __patient

c. __just

b. __mire

d. __together

4) Other prefixes to make words negative are *mis-* and *ir-*, which mean **wrong** and **not**. Use a dictionary to find five words containing these prefixes.

Links to writing

1) The prefix *mini-* means **small**. Add it to the following words to make new ones. Does the spelling of the root of the word change?

a. mum

c. bus

b. skirt

d. beast

2) The prefix *audi-* means to **hear** and *aqua-* means **water**. Find at least three words containing each of these prefixes.

3) Make a set of rules to display in your classroom which gives spelling hints to use when you are transforming words with prefixes.

3 Transforming words – suffixes

Suffixes go at the end of words to change their meaning.

You can make things more or less than they are.

simple

simple **-er**

simple **-est**

deep

deep **-er**

deep **-est**

kind

kind **-er**

kind **-est**

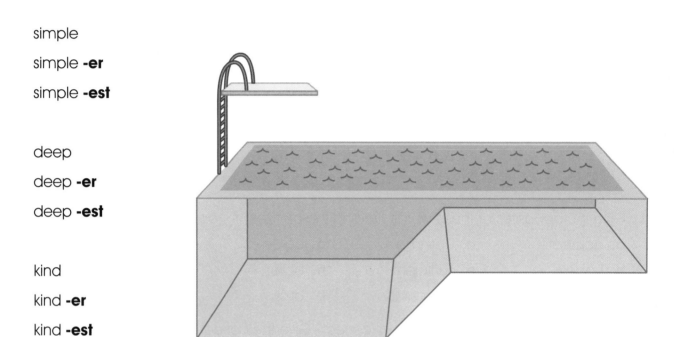

You can change one kind of word into another.

Verb	Noun
to educate	educat – ion
to criticise	critic – ism

Noun	Verb
light	to light – en
magnet	to magnet – ise
simplicity	to simpl – ify

Chat challenge

What is a suffix?

If you add a suffix to the end of a word, does it change the spelling of the original root of the word?

Can you think of any examples?

How is a suffix different from a prefix?

Do you know any tricks for learning to spell words where suffixes have been added?

How can some suffixes change the meaning of a word?

Comprehension

1) Identify the suffixes in the words on the opposite page.

2) Identify the root form of these words.

3) When you add a suffix to the root form of the word to change the word form (e.g. verb to noun), does the spelling of the word change? How?

4) Break the words opposite down into their syllables, e.g. ed – u – cat – ion.

5) Do you know any rules that would help when adding suffixes? What happens, for instance, if you have to add a suffix to a word ending in -e?

Objective focus

1) Make comparisons between the following words by adding suffixes, following the pattern on the opposite page.

   a. small   **c.** tall   **e.** straight
   b. fine   **d.** chewy   **f.** hot

   What changes do you have to make in the spelling of the words?

2) Some words do not use suffixes to make them mean **more** or **less**. Write the correct versions of the following words.

   a. beautifuller   beautifullest   **b.** thoughtfuller   thoughtfullest
   c. interestinger   interestingest

   Write a rule to help you to remember how to use **more** or **most** with these longer words.

Links to writing

1) There are other ways of transforming words. Form nouns from the following adjectives.

   a. loyal   **b.** good   **c.** high

   What changes do you notice in the spelling of the words?

2) Form verbs from the following nouns.

   a. knee   **b.** spark   **c.** clean

   What changes do you notice in the spelling of the words?

3) Make a poster to display in your classroom which gives spelling hints when you are using suffixes to transform words. Use a computer to do this. You could make the suffixes a different colour or highlight the letters in the words that change when you add a suffix.

4 Spelling patterns in plurals

Plurals are used to show that there is more than one of something.

dog + dog = dogs

sister + sister = sisters

school + school = schools

donkey + donkey = donkeys

monkey + monkey = monkeys

BUT

bus + bus = buses

church + church = churches

dish + dish = dishes

city + city = cities

baby + baby = babies

lorry + lorry = lorries

calf + calf = calves

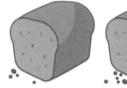

loaf + loaf = loaves

thief + thief = thieves

Chat challenge

What is a plural?

What does **singular** mean?

Which kinds of words can you change to the plural from the singular? Discuss whether you can change adjectives or verbs into plurals. Is it only nouns that can be made plural?

Talk about three common mistakes that writers make when trying to make plurals.

What tricks do you know for learning to spell plurals?

Comprehension

1) Which are the easiest kinds of plurals to make? Why? What is the simplest rule for making a plural?

2) What do you add when words end in *s*, *sh*, *ch*?

3) What do you add when words end in a consonant + *y*?

4) What do you add when words end in a vowel + *y*?

Objective focus

1) Give the plurals of these phrases:

    a. a goose and a sheep   **e.** a lorry in a city

    b. a mouse and a deer   **f.** a hiss and a cry

    c. a child and a woman   **g.** a potato and a tomato

    d. a fox in a box   **h.** a radio on the patio

2) Explain to someone who does not speak English how to make the plurals of the following.

    gas   latch   duty   country   donkey   monkey   house   six   wife

    potato   fireman   glass   fly   ash   knife   party   class   penny

Links to writing

1) Some plurals are tricky. Find the plurals of these words:

    a. stereo   **c.** studio   **e.** tomato

    b. patio   **d.** potato   **f.** volcano

    Check your answers in a dictionary.

2) Which of the following is the correct plural? Check your answers in a dictionary.

    a. teethbrush   toothbrushes   teethbrushes

    b. persons   people   personable

    c. aircraft   aircrafts   airs-craft

    d. gooses   geeses   geese

    e. sheep   sheeps   shoop

3) Make a book for your classroom which gives spelling hints when you are making plurals. Use a computer to do this. Use pictures to make it fun.

5 Grouping words according to meaning

You can group some words because they contain the same prefix.

The prefix will probably come from Latin or Greek. It should help you with the meaning of the word.

auto	autograph autobiography	(*auto*- means **self**)
circ	circulate circle	(*circus*- means **circle**)
bi	bisect bicycle	(*bi*- means **two**)
tele	telephone television	(*tele*- means **from afar**)

Some words contain a root of an ancient word.

This will help you to group them.

graph photograph	(*graphein* is an ancient Greek word meaning **to write**)
microscope microlight	(*micros*- is an ancient Greek word meaning **small**)
decimal decade	(*dec*- comes from the Greek word *deka* meaning **ten**)

Chat challenge

Many English words come from other languages. Which languages do you think have had the biggest effect on English?

What does **derivation** mean?

How can knowing the derivation of words help you to spell them?

Where might you find out more about the derivation of words and how this can help you with spelling?

Which parts of words make it easier for you to group words: beginnings (prefixes), middles (roots) or ends (suffixes)?

Comprehension

1) Some words in this section are very difficult. Write down the meanings of all the words, using a dictionary when necessary.

2) Why is it helpful to know something of the derivation of words if you want to group them?

3) Break the words opposite down into syllables. This will make you concentrate on one part of the word at a time. Do you recognise any patterns in your groups?

4) Separate the prefixes from the roots of the words. Which words do you recognise? Can you guess what their prefixes mean, e.g. how many wheels does a bicycle have?

5) Does your dictionary say anything about where the words originally came from?

Objective focus

1) Find some more words that you could add to groups of words containing the prefixes opposite, e.g. **auto circ bi tele trans**

2) The prefix *con-* means **together**. Say what these words mean.

    a. congregation   **b.** connect   **c.** constellation

3) Make as many words as you can with each of the following prefixes. Their meaning is in brackets.

    a. *uni-* (one)   **b.** *tri-* (three)   **c.** *quad-* (four)

4) Find one word beginning with *ex-* for each of the following.

    a. to cry out   **c.** to trade goods with another country

    b. to breathe out   **d.** to put out a fire

Links to writing

1) *Micro* comes from a Greek word meaning **small**. Use a dictionary and find three words to group containing this root.

2) *Manu* comes from a Latin word meaning **hand**. Use a dictionary and find three words to group containing this root.

3) Use all these words in sentences to show that you know what they mean.

4) Give one word beginning with *sur-* for each of the following:

    a. the top of the water   **c.** a person who escapes from a shipwreck

    b. to give in during a fight   **d.** an amount of something that is left over

Assess your
understanding

 OK

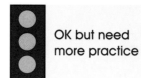 OK but need
more practice

 not at all clear
and need to
revisit

6 What have we learned?

We've learned about **word structure and spelling**.

1 How to spell words that have unstressed vowels in them

- Sometimes unstressed vowels are missed out altogether **in speech** (e.g. **different** – where we hardly hear the middle e).

- Made-up sayings (*mnemonics*) can help us to remember how to spell words that have unstressed vowels (e.g. because – **b**ig **e**lephants **c**an **a**lways **u**nderstand **s**mall **e**lephants).

- Thinking about word families and related words can help us choose the correct unstressed vowel – **gramm**a**tical** helps you to know that the unstressed vowel in **gramm**a**r** is an *a*.

Check understanding!

Check a piece of your own recent written work and look for unstressed vowel spelling errors.

2 How prefixes can transform words

- A prefix is a letter pattern fixed to the beginning of a word which affects its meaning.

- If you know what the prefix means it can help you to work out the meaning of an unknown word and how to spell it.

- Some prefixes are short, e.g. *bi-* and some are longer, e.g. *auto*.

Check understanding!

Read the points above again.
When you find a new prefix, make a note of it in a list and jot down its meaning, so that you can use it again. Begin the list now with five examples.

Assess your
understanding OK   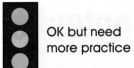 OK but need
more practice    not at all clear
and need to
revisit

3 How suffixes can transform words

Use your lists

- A suffix is a letter pattern fixed to the end of a word which affects its meaning.

- Some suffixes begin with a consonant, e.g. *-ment*; some suffixes begin with a vowel, e.g. *-ion*.

Check understanding!

 Keep a list of consonant and vowel suffixes; start it now by writing the rule for adding a consonant suffix, and the rule for adding a vowel suffix.

4 How to sort words by looking at spelling patterns

- **Singular** means one and **plural** means more than one.

- There are groups of words that:

  add -s (dogs)   **change y to i and add -es (cities)**

  add -es (dishes)   **change f to v and add -es (loaves)**

  don't follow rules! (geese)

- Simple plurals don't need an apostrophe.

Check understanding!

 Keep a list of words under the different types of plurals. Start it now and give another example for each.

5 How to sort words by looking at meaning

- **Derivation** means 'where something has come from'.

- Many prefixes come from Ancient Greek or Latin; once you know this it can help you to sort words and guess meanings.

Check understanding!

 Keep a list of words that derive from Greek and those from Latin. Start it now and give five examples for each.

7 Making notes to explain things

People in ancient times supposed that the Earth was something like a flat disc, surrounded by a 'moat' of ocean, over which rotated the star-spangled dome of the heavens. Beyond the moat were huge mountains which supported the heavens. Beyond the dome was a heaven composed of water – some of which came down as rain, through trap doors. The sun, as a god in his chariot, crossed the sky every day. Below the Earth was Hades, the place for the dead – also surrounded by water.

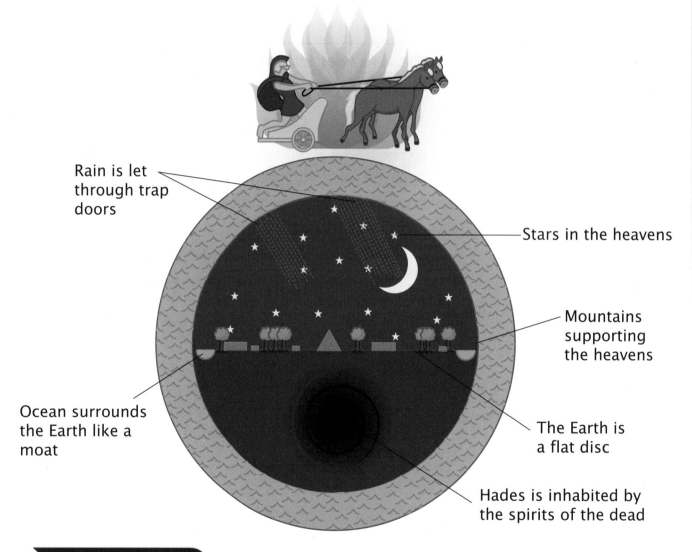

Rain is let through trap doors

Stars in the heavens

Mountains supporting the heavens

Ocean surrounds the Earth like a moat

The Earth is a flat disc

Hades is inhabited by the spirits of the dead

Chat challenge

Why do people make notes?
What notes do you make at home?
What notes do you make at school?
How can a diagram be more useful than a page of words?
Would the diagram be as useful if there were no labels?
In what way is this picture of the world different from the one you learn about in geography?

Comprehension

1) What shape did people in ancient times think the world was?

2) What did they think it was surrounded by?

3) How did they think the rain was caused?

4) Where did they think the sunlight came from?

5) How did they explain the heavens not falling down?

6) What did they believe was underneath the Earth?

Objective focus

1) Find the text in the passage for which labels are given in the diagram. Is anything missed out? Which is easier to understand – the passage of text or the diagram? Why?

2) Here are some notes from a shopping list. Write them out in at least four sentences, as a paragraph, starting 'You will need …'. Decide which version – the notes or the paragraph – is best for its purpose. Why?

3) Make notes from the passage on the opposite page, using abbreviations, to produce a shorter version as a paragraph. Is this easier to understand than the diagram given?

Links to writing

1) Read through the passage opposite and pick out the most important (key) words. Write these down and use them as the centre of a spider diagram to which you can add notes. Underline key words in colour on your diagram.

2) It is important that you put notes into your own words. Write out the notes on the diagram in your own words, finding different words for **heavens**, **supporting**, **disc**, **inhabited**, **surrounds**, **ocean**.

3) Ask yourself questions about a passage from a geography or a history book you are using in class. Who? What? Where? When? Why? Your answers will be the notes.

8 Writers' perspectives

The Runner

It wasn't running away. Not proper running away. Not really.

The monster Intercity hauled itself into the station. Jason was already at the edge of the platform with his bag in his hand. The other waiting passengers crowded around him as the train slowed. He kept his head low, scared someone might recognise him, and gripped the handles of his bag tighter. It felt so very heavy, it seemed to be dragging him down. Could he really carry it all the way to Liverpool? After as many as eight or nine carriages the train finally managed to bring itself to a halt. It still had another two or three to go but left them hanging out of the station, like a tall man in a small bed. The straggly crowd was an excuse not to queue and Jason was the last to climb aboard, even though he'd been one of the first waiting.

He followed the crowds on the train and grabbed the first empty seat he came to. Then almost immediately wished he hadn't. Sitting across the aisle from him was an elderly woman with a bag of mint imperials and a wrinkly smile. She offered him first the smile, then a sweet. He shook his head quickly and hurried through to the next carriage along, lugging his bag behind him.

Keith Gray

Chat challenge

Why might Jason be running away?

Try to visualise Jason standing on the platform.

Try to empathise with Jason – if you were running away how would you feel? Happy? Scared? Both?

Try to predict where he decides to sit.

Do these techniques help you to understand the text better?

What do you think? Is running away from home brave or foolish?

What things might Jason have in his bag?

If you were a writer, how would you make the feelings of your character known to your reader? By telling them directly? By showing them through what he says and does? Which do you think is the best way?

Comprehension

1) What do the first three sentences tell you about how the writer wants us to feel about Jason?

2) How is he travelling?

3) Why does he stand right at the edge of the platform as the train arrives?

4) Where is he going?

5) How many carriages manage to fit into the station?

6) Is there anything strange in the old woman's behaviour?

Objective focus

1) Look closely at the description of the train. Pick out some details that show the train as something alive. Why do you think the author does this?

2) Find some details from the passage to show that Jason was trying not to be noticed.

3) How does the way he handled his bag show that he was nervous?

4) Find a sentence to show that he was not certain that he could run away successfully.

5) Look closely at Jason's reaction to other people. List some details. What does the writer want you to understand from these?

Links to writing

1) The passage opens with three short sentences. Who is speaking here?

2) Imagine that you have to tell an untruth to protect someone. Write the opening paragraphs of a story, showing how you feel. Begin with: 'It wasn't lying. Not proper lying anyway. Not really.'

3) Identify three powerful verbs in the passage, e.g. **lugging**. (The writer could have used another word, e.g. **carried**, but this would not have given an impression of how heavy the bag seemed to Jason.) Find a weaker verb the writer could have used instead of each of the three verbs. Say why the stronger verb is better.

4) Plan and write a story in which a character is running away. Show how the character feels by what he or she says and by what he or she does. Use the same kind of detail as in the passage. Use a computer and edit on screen.

9 Structure of narrative texts – beginnings

Buried Alive

'I think it's a super castle,' said Biscuits. 'Truly. A fantastic creation. Practically the eighth wonder of the world. Honest, Tim.'

'Ooooh! Let's see this super-duper castle, eh?' said a loud voice behind us, making us both jump.

Two boys had crept up behind us. One was about our age and very pale and pinched-looking. He didn't look very tough but his smile was spiteful. He was the sort of boy you treated with caution.

The other boy was much bigger. And much tougher too. His hair was shaved so short it was just prickles, which looked as sharp as spikes. If he head-butted you you'd get severely perforated. He was the sort of boy that made a Red Alert system buzz inside your brain.

He was wearing great big Doc Martens even on the beach. I looked at the boy. I looked at the boots. I knew what was going to happen next.

'What a dinky ducky castle you two little cissy boys have made,' he said, his eyes beady. 'Shame it's just sand. Someone could accidentally trip and …'

He kicked hard. The castle collapsed.

Jacqueline Wilson

Chat challenge

Why are the beginnings of stories so important?
How does starting a story with speech impact on the story?
How much information should the writer give about characters at the beginning of a story?
The first page of a story can start at the end of the story! How can this be?
Think about books you have enjoyed recently. What type of beginnings do you like?
What's a really boring way to start a story? Over the next few weeks, make a class record of some story starts.

Comprehension

1) How does the title of the story help you to understand what follows? Where do you think the story is set? Why?

2) Which characters are named in the first paragraph?

3) Why do both characters jump?

4) What did the two other boys look like?

5) Why was one of them the sort who 'made a Red Alert system buzz in your brain'?

6) Did **you** know 'what was going to happen next'? Why?

Objective focus

1) What kind of people are Biscuits and Tim? What words or actions tell you this?

2) What does 'Ooooh!' tell you about how the character really felt? Why did he use words like 'super-duper'?

3) What does the verb 'crept' tell you about how the characters moved? What impression does it give you about them?

4) What impression would these verbs give you if they were used to describe people?
    a. stagger (not walk)   **c.** nibble (not eat)
    b. slurp (not drink)   **d.** grasp (not hold)

5) Find some details in the descriptions of the characters which show that they are not meant to be liked, e.g. **smile**, **clothing** and **hair style**.

6) What do you think happens next in the story? How would Tim and Biscuits react?

Links to writing

1) Write the ending of the story, but as if it was all a misunderstanding and the characters were not as nasty as they seem.

2) Write a story about bullying, making the opening similar to the one in the passage. Start with speech. Create some characters. Give details about the following.
    a. what he/she looks like
    b. what he/she says
    c. what he/she does

Use descriptive verbs to make the action more exciting.

10 Structure of narrative texts – story structure

Dennis the Menace

© D.C. Thomson & Co. Ltd.

Chat challenge

Stories should at least have a beginning, middle and end. Try to work with a beginning, a build up, a problem, a resolution and an end. Which part do you think this extract comes from?

What clues are there to tell you this?

What would happen if a story did not have a build up?

Would you be happy if a story did not have a resolution?

Cartoons use very few words to tell a story. How else do they give you a sense of what is going on?

Think about the 'theme' of Dennis the Menace. How many other characters can you think of that are like this sort of character and have this sort of theme?

Comprehension

1) Who are the main characters in this story?

2) Give some evidence to show that the story starts with some action.

3) What device in this cartoon makes the story develop?

4) What is going to happen next?

5) How do you think it will end?

Objective focus

1) Continue the story in note form to make sure that you have a beginning, an extended middle and an end.

2) Cartoons are similar to **storyboards**. Plan out the story of a well-known fairy tale using only six pictures. Decide on the most important events and characters and what the order of the story should be.

3) Stories need conflict or problems – something needs to happen to make the character do something. Choose three well-known children's stories and write about the conflict in them. What does the main character do to overcome the problem? Do characters always win in the end?

Links to writing

1) Here is a story with a structure.

   Once upon a time, there was a thirsty man on a sofa. He got up off the sofa, went to his kitchen, searched through his refrigerator, found a bottle of water, drank it, and returned to his seat, thirst quenched.

   What is wrong with this story?

2) Improve on the story. Start by asking yourself some questions about your main character, what might happen to him and how he will react.

   Who is your main character?

   What does your character look like?

   What is your character's personality?

   What will happen to your character and how will he react?

3) Now start adding other information. If you are using a computer you can use the following list as a guide and edit, add and move text around on screen.

   Action   background   Conflict   development   end

11 Structure of narrative texts – endings

How Comes that Blood? A ballad

'How comes that blood all over your shirt?
My son, come tell to me.'
'It's the blood of my good and friendly horse –
O mother, please let me be.'

'Your horse's blood is not so red.
My son, come tell to me.'
'It's the blood of my little hunting dog
That played in the field with me …'

'Your dog lies over there my son,
And this it could not be.'
'It is the blood of my old strong ox
That pulled the plough for me.'

'How comes the blood all over your shirt?
My son, you must tell to me.'
'It's the blood of my little brother Bill
Who I killed in the field today …'

'And what will you do when your father comes home?
My son, come tell it to me.'
'I'll put my feet in the bottom of a boat
And sail across the sea.'

Anon

Chat challenge

Why are endings important when you are telling a story?
How would you feel if a story you were reading did not have an ending?
If you just read the end of this 'story', would it make sense? Why not?
Stories should have a beginning, a developed middle and an end. Does it make any difference that this is a poem?
What do you find more difficult about reading a story in the form of a poem?
Think of other examples of texts that have the same theme (e.g. death) but aren't poetry – non-fiction, fiction, film, play …

Comprehension

1) Who are the two characters speaking in this poem? How do you know?

2) What is the story really about?

3) What kind of excuses does the son give?

4) How do we know that his mother does not believe him?

5) Why do you think the son wants to be 'let be'?

6) Whose blood is on his shirt? Why is he telling so many lies?

7) Does the ending come as a shock? Why?

8) How does this story end? What does he have to do before his father returns?

Objective focus

1) List what happens in each of the five verses of the poem.

2) What sort of pattern can you see in the way that the story is written?

3) Which verses would you say contain the beginning, the middle and the end of the story?

4) Tell the story of the first verse of the poem only. How can you make more of the setting, the characters and what they say and do?

5) How does the story build up to the tense moment when the son tells his mother what he did?

Links to writing

1) Write the story in a different way, so that the ending is different, as if it is true that the blood is from his horse. Think about how he could prove his mother wrong every time she questions him.

2) What would happen if he stayed to meet his father? Continue the story and explain how and why he killed his brother.

3) Write paragraphs using a computer. Split up your lines to make it look like a poem. What difference does it make to the telling of the story?

4) Find some more old ballads using the Internet. Look at the stories they contain and see how they end.

12 News reports

Headline – the main idea of the report

Fred's ruler destroyed as it topples from table

Opening – Who? What? Where?

Today at a small city primary school, there was confusion and shock when a ruler toppled from a table and smashed on the floor.

Body of text – the details

The ruler, a new plastic one especially purchased for school to use in literacy class, belonged to short-haired Fred Savage – a Year 5 student at Admiral House Primary School in Docklands, and is now totally useless.

Subheadings – key events

Knocked flying

Other opinions – include quotations

When interviewed Fred stated, 'I'm in shock. It happened this morning. I was just starting to think about writing my story so I looked for my new ruler. It had disappeared.' He paused for a moment to recover his thoughts. The shocked and shaken Fred continued. 'Then I saw it on the table. I was relieved because I thought my friends were playing a joke. Suddenly, as I stood up, the books fell sideways and knocked it flying. I could do nothing about it.'

Year 4 boys to be interviewed

Fred's best mate, Andy – a lively dark-haired sporty type, also in Year 5, told us in confidence that he thought the opposing football team in Year 4 must have deliberately positioned the books so this would happen. 'Fred is our best scorer and they knew he would be upset for the game tomorrow. How low can you sink?' he sneered accusingly.

Style – past tense; detail about who, what, when, where, how. Brief, catchy detail

Fred's teacher, Ms Smith (32 with long blonde hair), said that she was looking into the complaints by members of her class and would be interviewing certain Year 4 boys. The class was still in a state of shock, but the school has issued a request to the general public for anyone who knows more about this distressing matter to contact them as soon as possible.

Chat challenge

What is the purpose of a newspaper report?

Who is the reader?

Why are headlines and subheadings important?

Look for verbs describing actions. Why do they have to be so accurate?

Would a photograph help? Why?

Do you know if everything you read in a newspaper report is true?

Comprehension

1) Where did this event occur?

2) When did this event occur?

3) Whose ruler was it?

4) What detail shows you that Fred was shocked?

5) Who was a witness to the event?

6) What is Andy's opinion of what happened?

7) How did the teacher react?

8) Is the report written in correct time order (from the beginning to the end of the story)? Find evidence to support your answer.

Objective focus

1) Write some more headlines for this story giving different views – was it the fault of Year 4, or someone else?

2) Find examples of headlines in other newspapers and say if you think they summarise the news story well.

3) Look at the style features of a newspaper report on the opposite page. Pick out examples of each.

4) Write the article as if by someone from Year 4. Look at the style hints. How would it be different?

5) Collect examples from the newspapers of articles about sports or pop stars. Work out why newspapers have published them.

Links to writing

1) Think of an important sports fixture. Write a report for the school newspaper as if you were there. Consider the following details.
   How will you introduce the scene? Who? What? Where? When? How? Why?
   What information will you include?
   Avoid using 'I' or 'me'.
   Whom will you interview and quote?

2) Use a computer to produce the newspaper article so that it looks like the real thing.

13 Instructions

CHOCOLATE BISCUITS

Get organised to make these wonderfully tasty chocolate biscuits in no time at all.

What you need

> **Materials or requirements to complete the task**

- ½ cup of self-raising flour
- 1½ teaspoons baking powder
- pinch of salt
- ½ cup of butter or margarine
- ½ cup of sugar

- 2 cups of grated chocolate
- 1 egg
- ½ cup of milk
- some cups for measuring
- 2 mixing bowls
- a fork
- a greased baking tray

What you do

> **What is the aim of the instructions?**

1 Mix together the flour, baking powder and salt in a mixing bowl.

2 Add the butter and use a fork to mix the ingredients together.

3 Stir in the sugar and grated chocolate.

> **Style – command verbs; use you; use connectives to do with time – then, first, now; be brief**

4 In another bowl, beat an egg thoroughly with a fork.

5 Add the milk to the egg and mix them together.

6 Pour the mixture of egg and milk into the flour mixture.

7 With your hands, knead the mixture lightly into a dough. If the mixture is very dry, add some more milk.

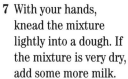
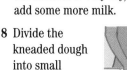

8 Divide the kneaded dough into small rounds.

9 Place the rounds on the greased baking tray.

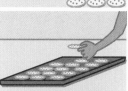

10 Bake the biscuits in a hot oven until done (approximately 20 minutes).

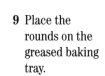
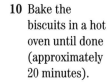

> **Evaluation – has it worked?**

After you have removed them from the tray, allow them to cool before eating. What do you think of them?

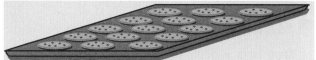

Chat challenge

What is the purpose of instructions?

Why is stating the aim of the instructions important?

If there were no materials or requirements stated, would the instructions work? Why?

Can any instructions be written in any order? Think of some examples.

What kind of verbs are used in instructions?

How do you know if instructions are good or not?

Comprehension

1) Why is a title useful in a set of instructions?

2) Why are subheadings useful? Write the sentences you would have to include if the subheadings were not there. What difference does it make?

3) What other features on the opposite page make the instructions easy to use?

4) What would happen if the steps were not in sequence?

 Objective focus

1) Look at the style features of the instructions on the opposite page. Pick out examples of each from the recipe.

2) Commands are used in instructions. Make a list of all the one-word commands that you would use if you were training a dog.

3) Write instructions for a two-player game, e.g. 'Stone, Paper, Scissors'. Usually commands are written using the **you** form of the verb. Use examples of the third person, e.g. 'Player 1' and 'Player 2'.

4) Write a set of simple numbered instructions, to help a young child tie shoelaces. You could draw diagrams to help.

 Links to writing

1) Imagine that you have a new pen friend from another country who is interested in what you do at school. Write instructions (written in simple English) to help him/her play a game or make something at school. Use these style tips.

Be brief and clear, but give all the right details.
Follow the right order.
Use link words (then, now) or numbers.
Use the present tense and command verbs.
Correct use of technical vocabulary.
The use of 'accurate' description – adjectives and adverbs in order to help the reader understand what to do.

14 Non-chronological reports

London

Basic facts

London is the capital city of the United Kingdom. It covers approximately 1600 km² and has a population of over nine million people. London is the largest city in the UK.

The city was founded by the Romans as Londinium in AD43. It was situated on a terrace near the north bank of the river Thames. The Thames is tidal, and so London has been a convenient port since this time.

London has mild winters (an average of 6°C) in January. Summers are not known to be very hot with an average of 21°C. The average rainfall is 600 mm. This is heaviest in the autumn months.

What to see in London

London is packed with things to see and do – and it's all too easy to miss things.

Museums

National museums in London are usually free. In the Natural History Museum are the skeletons of dinosaurs. Tate Britain and Tate Modern show the national collection of British paintings from the 16th century to today. Older paintings are held in the National Gallery.

Historic buildings

Everywhere in London are famous buildings reflecting the history of the city: the Tower of London, the Houses of Parliament, Guild Hall.

Entertainment

Theatre and cinema can be found in Leicester Square and Shaftesbury Avenue in the West End. Shakespeare's Globe theatre is on the south bank of the Thames. To get away from the crowds, visit any of London's parks such as Hyde Park and Regent's Park.

So, whatever the weather, make sure that you plan your day in London to make the most of your visit.

General opening – the facts

Set out using subheadings to make information clearer to read

Style – present tense; third person; linking verbs (is the, has a)

The report is ordered by a scheme – but not in time sequence

Chat challenge

What is the purpose of a report?

Where would you find a report like this?

Discuss where the text shifts from being a straight report to a report with persuasive elements.

Would you write in this style at school? If so, in what subjects?

How is the report set out differently from other reports? Why?

Many reports follow a sequence of events in time order (chronological). Why does this one not need to?

Comprehension

1) How large is London in area and how many people live there?

2) Who founded the city? How can you tell from the use of its original name?

3) Which river runs through the city?

4) Where can you see the best collection of modern art?

5) Where would you go if you wanted to see dinosaur skeletons?

6) Where is Shakespeare's theatre to be found?

Objective focus

1) What is the purpose of this report? Who is the intended audience?

2) Which person of the verb is used that tells you this? Write down three examples.

3) Rewrite the report from 'What to see ...' using the second person of the verb – **you**. What difference does it make?

4) Which topics does the writer use to help organise his/her work?

5) Write the sentences you would use to introduce each paragraph if you did not use subheadings. What difference does this make?

Links to writing

1) Write a weekly report about how you look after a pet, such as a cat or a dog, day by day. How is this different from a non-chronological report?

2) Write a non-chronological report about an animal you have studied in class. How do you house it? What do you feed it? What is important to remember when looking after it?

3) Write a non-chronological report about a place that you have visited on holiday.

   Decide which place and then list what makes it interesting.

   Find out facts about the place. Use the Internet.

   Write subheadings to help you organise your work.

   Write in paragraphs.

   Do not use words such as *I* or *we*.

   Check your final version against the style tips in the boxes beside the text on the opposite page.

   Find pictures from the Internet to illustrate the report. Publish it.

15 Letters

Admiral House Primary School has been told that its local playing field is to be sold.
New houses will be built on it.

Admiral House Primary School
Docklands
Liverpool
19 January

Your address here with the date

The address of the person to whom you are sending this

The Managing Director
Customer Builders
Stonard Road
Manchester

Dear Sir,
I am writing to tell you that my whole class (5B) is upset by the fact that you want to build houses on our playing field.
We all enjoy PE and games and this playing field is the only place the school has to carry out these activities. Where are we going to go when the houses have been built?
Our teacher says that it is the law to teach PE but we will have nowhere to do this. We will have to hire a coach to get to a playing field miles away. This will be very expensive for our school and we are not very well off.
What is more, we will also have to share this field with two other schools so we will not have so much time. Think of all the hours travelling in London traffic. This will mean we can spend less time doing important things like literacy.
My mum says she will not be able to pick me up from this field after school because it is too far away from where she works. Other children in my class have the same problems.
I hope you can understand our point of view and will reconsider your plans.

Yours faithfully,
Dominic

!!SAVE OUR SCHOOL PLAYING FIELD!!

Each paragraph contains one argument

Persuasive language: what is more … using questions

Formal greeting and ending

Chat challenge

What is the purpose of this letter?

How is it different from a letter you would send to a friend?

What features of style would you **not** use for such a letter? Why?

If you are trying to persuade someone, what are the best ways of doing this in writing?

Has the writer persuaded you? Why?

English Study Guide: Year 5

Answer Booklet

1 Unstressed vowels
Comprehension
1) poisonous, separate, extraordinary, conference, stationery, definitely, secretary, interested, business, Wednesday
2) poi–son–ous, sep–a–rate, ex–tra–ord–in–ary, con–fer–ence, sta–tion–ery, de–fi–nit–ely, sec–re–tary, in–ter–es–ted, bus–i–ness, Wed–nes–day
3) extraordinary, definitely, interested
4) Every syllable contains a vowel.
5) You give it emphasis over the rest of the word.
6) You might sound silly (like a robot)!

Objective focus
1) animal, dictionary, generally, library, marvellous
2) description, difference, generous, interest, miserable
3) **a.** different
   b. factory
   c. desperate
   d. definite
   e. hospital
4) d(i)f–f(e)r–(e)nt
   f(a)c–t(o)r–y
   d(e)s–p(e)r–(a)t(e)
   d(e)f–(i)n–(i)t(e)
   h(o)s–p(i)–t(a)l

Links to writing
1) *Own answer*
2) Break the words into syllables.
3) *Own answer*

2 Transforming words – prefixes
Comprehension
1) im-, il-, un-, ad-, re-, al-
2) -mature, -practical, -literate, -legal, -believable, -happy, -vance, -dition, -turn, -animate, -mighty, -most
3) Whole words: turn, animate, mighty, most, mature, practical, literate, legal, believable, happy
   Parts of words: vance, dition
4) Generally, adding a prefix to a word does not change its spelling.
5) *Own answer*

Objective focus
1) **a.** inaccurate
   b. unhappy
   c. unable or disable
   d. uncommon
   e. insufficient
   f. unnecessary
   g. disagree
   h. disbelief
   i. disallow
   j. discontinue
   k. inattentive
   l. disown
2) **a.** impossible
   c. unimaginable
3) **a.** impatient

b. admire
c. unjust
d. altogether
4) *Own answer*

Links to writing
1) No, the spelling stays the same.
   a. minimum
   b. miniskirt
   c. minibus
   d. minibeast
2), 3) *Own answers*

3 Transforming words – suffixes
Comprehension
1) -er, -est, -ion, -ism, -en, -ise, -ify
2) simple-, deep-, kind-, educate-, criticise-, light-, magnet-, simplicity-
3) In most cases the spelling of the word doesn't change, but in many cases it does. The final, silent e is lost in words when adding a suffix beginning with a vowel. The final y becomes an i.
4) sim–ple, sim–pler, sim–plest
   keep, deep–er, deep–est
   kind, kind–er, kind–est
   ed–u–cate, ed–u–ca–tion
   cri–ti–cise, cri–ti–cism
   light, light–en
   mag–net, mag–net–ise
   sim–pli–ci–ty, sim–pli–fy
5) **a.** When you add y or a suffix that begins with a vowel to words ending in a silent e, you drop the e and add the suffix.
   b. When you add suffixes to words that end in ge or ce, do not drop the final e.
   c. The ending ing is a verb ending. When you add ing to words that end in ie, you drop the e and change the y to i. Then you add ing.
   d. When you add suffixes that do not end in vowels or y, you do not drop the final e.
   e. When you add suffixes that begin with a consonant, keep the final e if the suffix begins with a consonant.
   f. When you add the suffix ment to a word, the final e is dropped.
   g. There are always exceptions to rules!

Objective focus
1) **a.** small, smaller, smallest (just added suffix)
   b. fine, finer, finest (removed final e and added suffix)
   c. tall, taller, tallest (just added suffix)
   d. chewy, chewier, chewiest (changed y to i and added suffix)
   e. straight, straighter, straightest (just added suffix)
   f. hot, hotter, hottest (added second t and then suffix)
2) **a.** more beautiful, most beautiful
   b. more thoughtful, most thoughtful

c. more interesting, most interesting
   If the word is more than one syllable use **more** or **most** and don't change the spelling of the word.

Links to writing
1) **a.** loyalty
   b. goodness
   c. highness
   There is no change in the spelling of these words but they add a suffix.
2) **a.** to kneel
   b. to spark
   c. to clean
   There is no change in the spelling of these words.
3) *Own answer*

4 Spelling patterns in plurals
Comprehension
1) The easiest kinds of plurals to make are ones where you simply add an s.
2) Words that end in s, sh, ch add es.
3) Change the y to i before adding es.
4) Remove the vowel and add ies.

Objective focus
1) **a.** two geese and two sheep
   b. two mice and two deer
   c. two children and two women
   d. two foxes in two boxes
   e. two lorries in two cities
   f. two hisses and two cries
   g. two potatoes and two tomatoes
   h. two radios on two patios
2) *Own answer*

Links to writing
1) **a.** stereos
   b. patios
   c. studios
   d. potatoes
   e. tomatoes
   f. volcanoes
2) **a.** toothbrushes
   b. people or persons
   c. aircraft
   d. geese
   e. sheep
3) *Own answer*

5 Grouping words according to meaning
Comprehension
1) *Own answer*
2) The prefix might help you understand the meaning of the word.
3) aut–o–graph, aut–o–bi–og–ra–phy
   cir–cu–late, cir–cus
   bi–sect, bi–cy–cle
   tel–e–phone, tel–e–vis–ion
   graph, pho–to–graph
   mic–ro–scope, mic–ro–light
   dec–i–mal, dec–ade
   Own answer
4) -graph, -biography, -late, -sect, -cycle, -phone, -vision, -graph,

-scope, -light, -imal, -ade
Auto means 'self', **circum** means 'circle', **bi** means 'two', **tele** means 'from afar', **graphein** means 'to write', **micros** means 'small', **dec** means 'ten'
5) *Own answer*

Objective focus
1) *Own answer*
2) **a. Congregation** means an assembly of persons brought together for common religious worship.
   b. Connect means to join, link or fasten together.
   c. Constellation means an easily-recognised group of stars that appear to be located close together in the sky.
3) *Own answer*
4) a. exclaim
   b. exhale
   c. export
   d. extinguish

Links to writing
1), 2), 3) *Own answers*
4) a. surface
   b. surrender
   c. survivor
   d. surplus

7 Making notes to explain things
Comprehension
1) They thought the world was a flat disc.
2) They thought it was surrounded by a 'moat' of ocean.
3) They thought rain was water from heaven which came through trap doors.
4) They thought sunlight came from a god crossing the sky every day.
5) The heavens were supported by mountains.
6) Hades

Objective focus
1) There is no label for the sun, as a god in his chariot, and there is no water surrounding Hades.
2), 3) *Own answers*

Links to writing
1), 2), 3) *Own answers*

8 Writers' perspectives
Comprehension
1) He is trying to convince himself he isn't running away and thoughts are running through his head quickly.
2) He is taking an Intercity train.
3) He's keen to get on the train as quickly as possible.
4) He is going to Liverpool.
5) Eight or nine carriages manage to fit into the station.
6) No, the woman doesn't seem to behave strangely.

Objective focus
1) The writer describes the train as a 'monster', states that it 'hauled itself into the station' and writes the train is 'like a tall man in a small bed'. The writer does this to help the reader visualise the train.
2) 'Jason was already at the edge of the platform.'
   'He kept his head low, scared someone might recognise him.'
   'He hurried through to the next carriage.'
3) He gripped his bag tighter.

4) 'Could he really carry it all the way to Liverpool?'
5) 'Scared someone might recognise him' He refuses the old lady's sweets, says nothing and hurries off.
   The writer wants the reader to understand that Jason doesn't want to be recognised.

Links to writing
1) The writer
2), 3), 4) *Own answers*

9 Structure of narrative texts – beginnings
Comprehension
1) The title helps the reader understand that the castle might collapse.
   The story could be set on the beach because the children are playing in the sand.
2) Biscuits and Tim are named in the first paragraph.
3) They were surprised by the unexpected voice.
4) One boy was 'very pale and pinched-looking. He didn't look very tough but his smile was spiteful.'
   'The other boy was much bigger. And much tougher too. His hair was shaved so short it was just prickles, which looked as sharp as spikes.'
5) Because he looks dangerous.
6) Maybe. The title was the first clue to help you guess what might happen. The descriptions of the boys also reinforced the idea that they might kick down the castle.

Objective focus
1) The boys are well spoken, articulate and educated. Biscuits complements Tim by saying 'A fantastic creation. Practically the eighth wonder of the world.'
2) 'Ooooh!' tells you that the boy is being sarcastic. He uses 'super-duper' because he is making fun of the way Tim and Biscuits speak.
3) 'Crept' implies that he moved slowly and don't want to be heard. It might make us think they're sneaky and up to no good.
4) *Own answer*
5) 'loud voice'
   'very pale and pinched-looking'
   'his smile was spiteful'
   'the sort of boy you treated with caution'
   'tougher'
   'his hair was shaved'
   'looked as sharp as spikes'
   'wearing big Doc Martens even on the beach'
6) *Own answer*

Links to writing
1), 2) *Own answers*

10 Structure of narrative texts – story structure
Comprehension
1) Dennis the Menace and his dad.
2) The character shouts the instruction, 'Barricade the door!'
3) The story is divided into frames.
4) Dennis will attempt to solve the mystery.
5) Dennis will get into trouble but everything will end happily.

Objective focus
1), 2), 3) *Own answers*

Links to writing
1) There is no conflict.
2), 3) *Own answers*

11 Structure of narrative texts – endings
Comprehension
1) The two characters are a mother and son. She refers to him as her son and then refers to his father in the final verse.
2) One brother killing another.
3) He says the blood is his horse's, the hunting dog's and the strong ox's.
4) She keeps asking where the blood came from. She says the blood is the wrong colour for the horse and points out the hunting dog.
5) He doesn't want to tell where the blood really came from.
6) The blood on his shirt is his brother's. He is probably telling so many lies so that he doesn't get into trouble.
7) Yes, because the boy has murdered another human being, his brother.
8) The story ends with the boy saying he will run away before his father returns. He will find a boat and 'will sail across the sea.'

Objective focus
1) Verse 1: The boy says the blood came from the horse.
   Verse 2: The boy says the blood came from his little hunting dog.
   Verse 3: The boy says the blood came from his strong ox.
   Verse 4: The boy confesses it is his brother's blood.
   Verse 5: The boy says he will run away.
2) In each verse the mother asks a question and the boy replies.
3) The beginning is the first verse, the middle is verses 2, 3 and 4 and the last verse is the end.
4) *Own answer*
5) The boy keeps telling lies which the mother doesn't believe.

Links to writing
1), 2), 3), 4) *Own answers*

12 News reports
Comprehension
1) The event occurred at Admiral House primary school in Docklands.
2) Today
3) The ruler belonged to Fred Savage.
4) 'there was confusion and shock'
   When interviewed Fred stated, 'I'm in shock.'
   'The shocked and shaken Fred continued.'
   'The class was still in a state of shock'
5) Apparently, there were no witnesses.
6) Andy suspects the Year 4 football team must have 'deliberately positioned the books so this would happen.'
7) She is looking into complaints by members of her class and will be interviewing certain Year 4 boys.
8) Yes, we learn what happened, then the reactions, and finally the consequences.

Objective focus
1), 2), 3), 4), 5) *Own answers*

Links to writing
1), 2) *Own answers*

13 Instructions
Comprehension
1) The title clearly tells the reader what the instructions are for.
2) Subheadings are useful to break down the instructions into understandable sections. For example, 'You will need ½ cup of self-raising flour. You will need 1½ teaspoons baking powder. You will need a pinch of salt …' This clearly becomes repetitive and obscures the useful information.
3) The features in the instructions that make it easy to use include: bullet points, numbering, use of italics, diagrams and illustrations.
4) It would be impossible to make biscuits.

Objective focus
1), 2), 3), 4) *Own answers*

Links to writing
1) *Own answer*

14 Non-chronological reports
Comprehension
1) London covers 1600 km2 and has a population of over nine million.
2) The city was founded by Romans who called it 'Londinium', which is very similar to 'London'.
3) The River Thames runs through the city.
4) The best collection of modern art is at the Tate Modern.
5) You should go to the Natural History Museum.
6) Shakespeare's Globe theatre is on the south bank of the Thames.

Objective focus
1) The purpose of this report is to inform, explain and describe. The intended audience is people want to learn more about London and people who may want to visit.
2) The third person is used in this text because it is impersonal, except in the final sentence when the reader is addressed directly as 'you'.
   Own answers
3) *Own answer*
4) The writer uses Basic Facts, Museums, Historic Buildings and Entertainment as topics to organise their work.
5) *Own answers*

Links to writing
1), 2), 3) *Own answers*

15 Letters
Comprehension
1) So that the person you wrote to knows who the letter has come from and how to get in contact with the writer.
2) The date is important because it allows the reader to place the letter in context of other events.
3) Dear Sir/Madam (when the writer is unsure of the recipient's gender and name)
   Dear Mr Smith (formal – when the person is known to the writer)
   Dear Claire (informal – when the person is know to the writer)
4) Yours faithfully (formal – when the person is unknown to the writer)
   Yours sincerely (formal – when the person is known to the writer)
   Yours truly (informal – when the person is known to the writer)

5) 'We all enjoy PE and games and this playing field is the only place the school has to carry out these activities.'
   'Our teachers say that it is the law to teach PE but we will have nowhere to do this.'
   'My mum says she will not be able to pick me up from this field after school because it is too far way from where she works.'
6) Dominic's tone is nice and polite.

Objective focus
1) The children enjoy PE and games.
   It is the law for the school to teach PE and it will cost the school a lot of money to transport the children to and from school.
   His mum will not be able to pick him up from the playing fields.
2) *Own answer*
3) a. Queen's Drive
      Belfast
      ABC 123
   b. Prince Walk
      London
      W3 4RR
   c. Water St
      Manchester
      1 2WW

Links to writing
1), 2) *Own answers*

16 Language for comic effect
Comprehension
1) Jokes 1, 2, 5, 6, 7, and 8 use puns.
2) Jokes 2, 7 and 9 depend upon the clever use of the sound of words.
3) They are homonyms which sound the same, but are spelled differently.
4) The words in the answer
5) The first letters from **takes** and **makes** are switched.
6) The author's names are homonyms which are related to the titles of the books.

Objective focus
1) a.–d. *Own answers*
2) a.–d. *Own answers*
3) a. hit
   b. back
   c. right

Links to writing
1), 2), 3) *Own answers*

18 Edit and improve your work
Comprehension
1) Little Wolf is writing this letter to let his parents know how things are going at school.
2) The school isn't open yet and Uncle Bigbad is being awkward.
3) Dad has a fang ache instead of a toothache. Also, Little Wolf says 'Paws crossed' instead of 'Fingers crossed'.
4) grrrish, soonly, wunce, orkwood
5) cross, soon, once, awkward
6) To emphasise them and bring them to the reader's attention or to mimic shouting in a verbal conversation.

Objective focus
1) a. I'll teach you. (wrong verb)
   b. You were the first. (the verb must agree with the subject)
   c. I don't know anything. (double negative)
   d. The book that I read. (**that** is

demonstrative but **what** is a question)
   e. He did it (the verb must agree with the subject)
2) a. She gave me. (incorrect tense, using present instead of past)
      or She gives me.
   b. the actors were (singular verb when it should be plural)
   c. My mum doesn't let us (plural verb when it should be singular)
   d. I never saw anyone (double negative)
   e. Tracey did her work (wrong tense)
3) I bet it's just because poor dad has fang ache.
4) *Own answer*

Links to writing
1), 2), 3), 4) *Own answers*

19 Adapt non-narrative forms and styles
Comprehension
1) The writer highlights the dangers of open windows.
2) To keep valuable objects safe from being broken by the kitten.
3) Kittens sleep up to 20 hours a day.
4) The kitten feels frightened when he arrives.
5) 'Lost in a big, big new world'
   'Snuggled in the palm of my hand'
   'When he sits on my shoulder'
6) The kitten is trembling because he is frightened.
7) Every line starts with **he**, followed by a verb to describe what the kitten **did** or **felt**.

Objective focus
1) The writer uses bullet points to break the information into understandable sections.
2) *Own answer*
3) No, reading the passage in any order makes sense. This is because a story isn't being told, information is being given.
4) a.–d. *Own answers*

Links to writing
1), 2), 3) *Own answers*

20 Viewpoint through the use of direct speech
Comprehension
1) A school playground in front of a brick wall.
2) Annie and Jack are sister and brother. We know this because 'Jack looked across the school playground at his sister.'
3) Annie seems to be talking to someone who isn't there.
4) Jack saw Annie nodding her head and smiling at the empty space next to her.
5) Her brother isn't surprised and doesn't particularly care what his sister does.
6) Annie is with her imaginary friend Sarah.
7) Annie's friend is an invisible time traveller.
8) Saying something in a sneering or cutting way.

Objective focus
1) New speaker, new paragraph
   Open and close speech marks
   Commas before speech starts
   Full stop or other final punctuation inside the speech marks
2) *Own answer*
3) Annie was nodding and smiling at her 'friend' so she was enjoying being with her. When she introduces her 'friend' to

Jack she has a pleased look on her face. Jack is embarrassed and fed up so he 'mutters' in reply. Annie 'retorted, unruffled' in reply to show that she doesn't care what Jack thinks. She 'opened her eyes wide and gave him a superior stare' to show that she knows best.

Links to writing
1), 2), 3) *Own answers*

21 Viewpoint through the use of action
Comprehension
1) The first thing he notices is that he has eyes on the sides of his head.
2) He finds it strange that his eyes don't focus together.
3) The locker reminds him of a long, grey field that wouldn't end because he is so small.
4) The words that tell us Jake is moving fast are: 'zoom' and 'flew'.
5) He compares his speed to an out-of-control missile.
6) Jake races after the spider because he is going to eat it.

Objective focus
1), 2), 3) *Own answers*

Links to writing
1), 2) *Own answers*

22 Viewpoint through the use of detail
Comprehension
1) The author describes his hat, face, clothes, jewellery and posture.
2) The author tells us the colour, size, shape of the features he describes.
3) The author uses interesting and unusual adjectives to describe these things.
4) 'He grinned a lot'
   'A habit of flopping his hand at you while he was talking'
   'Wriggling sort of chap'
5) 'Narrow eyes'
   'Bad teeth'
   'Perfectly ghastly tie'
6) He is dressed up like an eel, he has a foxy sort of face and his suit is like drawing room curtains.
7) The writer's description of the character makes the reader dislike him.

Objective focus
1), 2), 3), 4) *Own answers*

Links to writing
1), 2), 3) *Own answers*

24 Paragraphs and order
Comprehension
1) Before money was invented people had to buy and sell by exchanging things.
2) The problem with the system was that you had to find somebody who wanted what you had to exchange.
3) Blocks of salt, shells and beads have all been used as forms of money.
4) Money has been made out of gold, silver and copper.
5) The weight of a coin was important because the value of a coin depended on how much of the gold, silver or copper it contained.
6) Governments agree the value of a coin and that amount is stamped on it.

Objective focus
1) The topic sentences are the first sentence in each paragraph.
2) Each paragraph starts by mentioning a point in time, for example: before, even after, eventually, the next stage and today.
3) The text is written in a chronological narrative order. If you mix this order up, the passage no longer makes sense.
4) *Own answer*

Links to writing
1), 2) *Own answer*

25 Changing the order of sentences
Comprehension
1) People were given surnames to help tell apart two people with the same first name. This information is in paragraph 3.
2) The word surname comes from the prefix *sur-* meaning 'over and above' or 'additional to'. This information is in paragraph 1.
3) Surnames were formed from either occupational names (paragraph 2) or from natural features (paragraph 3).
4) **a.** Johnson, because it is not an occupation.
   b. Brook, because it is not an occupation (Baxter means 'baker')
   c. Smith, because it is not a natural feature.

Objective focus
1) Every other Monday I go to my Club, but we are moving soon to a new house. I think I will have to stop going because of the journey.
   It would be pleasant in summer but not good in winter, when the nights are cold and dark; especially if you like sitting in front of the TV like me.
2) The writer begins the paragraph with a question to introduce the main topic of the paragraph and make the reader think about the answer themselves. The other sentences in the paragraph go on to answer the question by giving further information and examples.
3) The order of sentences is important to guide the reader through the text logically.

Links to writing
1), 2), 3) *Own answers*

26 Speech marks
Comprehension
1) The two characters speaking in the passage are Tom Sawyer and Huck Finn.
2) They've met by the dead tree because they had come for their tools.
3) They don't go to the house because it is a Friday.
4) Their view of Friday is that it is an unlucky day.
5) This seems strange because it is very superstitious.
6) Huck had a dream about rats which also concerned them.
7) The reader knows who is speaking each time because every time there is a new speaker a new paragraph is started.

Objective focus
1) New speaker, new paragraph
   Open and close speech marks
   Commas before speech starts
   Full stop or other final punctuation inside

the speech marks.
2) 'Look out!' warned the passenger.
   'What's the matter?' muttered the driver, half asleep.
   'Sorry,' the passenger answered apologetically, 'I thought you were going to crash.'
3) *Own answer*

Links to writing
1) 'There's some lucky days, maybe, but Friday ain't.'
   Some days of the week are lucky, but Friday is not.
   By using standard English rather than non-standard English you lose the character's way of speaking and, therefore, their personality.
2), 3) *Own answer*

27 Apostrophes
Comprehension
1) The only two knights left are Sir Lucan and Sir Bedivere.
2) The two knights carried King Arthur to the deserted chapel in Camelot because he was dying.
3) King Arthur asks Sir Bedivere to take Excalibur and throw the sword into a lake.
4) When he tries to throw the sword away a voice persuades him not to.
5) He tells King Arthur that the water rippled when he threw the sword into the lake, but nothing else.
6) King Arthur is furious and calls Sir Bedivere a liar and a traitor.

Objective focus
1) **Letters left out**   **Showing possession**
   He'd   Camelot's castles
   We're   My time's short
   Don't   His knight's vows
2) **a.** can't
   b. it's
   c. what's
   d. I've
   e. they've
   f. they're
3) **a.** The picture's frame
   b. A dog's collar
   c. The two ships' anchors
   d. The ladies' dresses
   e. The author's book
   f. Many artists' paintings

Links to writing
1) **a.** The cat's kittens (one cat with lots of kittens)
      The cats' kittens (many cats with their kittens)
   b. My brother's books (the books belonging to one brother)
      My brothers' books (the books belonging to several brothers)
   c. The girl's dresses (the dresses belonging to one girl)
      The girls' dresses (the dresses belonging to several girls)
   d. The farmer's fields (the fields belonging to one farmer)
      The farmers' fields (the fields belonging to several farmers)
2) *Own answer*

Author: Andrew Plaistowe
Design: Clive Sutherland
Editorial: Dodi Beardshaw

Comprehension

1) Why is it important to put your address in a letter?

2) Why is the date important?

3) What ways are there to start a letter besides 'Dear Sir'? When would you use them?

4) What ways are there to end a letter besides 'Yours faithfully'? When would you use them?

5) List three arguments that Dominic uses to convince the builders.

6) Does Dominic sound nice or nasty in the tone of his writing?

Objective focus

1) List the arguments that the writer uses in this letter. Can you suggest some better ones?

2) In an argument you can use words or phrases to suggest an alternative. Use each of these in a sentence to show this.

   a. but   **c.** some people argue that

   b. however   **d.** could be argued that

3) Write out the following addresses as they should appear on a letter.

   a. queens drive Belfast abc 123

   b. prince walk London w3 4rr

   c. water st Manchester 1 2ww

Links to writing

1) Imagine you are the builders and you write a reply to Dominic's letter. Use the style tips'.

   What arguments would you use?

   Write a paragraph for each argument. Give examples.

   Set the letter out correctly.

   Use some of the words useful for arguments above.

2) Write the letter using a computer, print it and sign it. You could role-play the reaction in the class when the letter is received – what would your friends say to oppose the arguments?

16 Language for comic effect

JOKES

1 What do baby apes sleep in?

Apricots

2 Which horses keep late hours?

Nightmares

3 What's the difference between a poor man and a feather bed?

One is hard up and the other is soft down

4 What's the difference between an engine driver and a school teacher?

One minds trains and the other trains minds

5 Why are acrobats nice people?

They are always doing good turns

6 What happened when the wheel was invented?

It caused a revolution

7 When is a book like a strawberry?

When it's red (read)

8 What do you call a building with lots of storeys?

A library

9 What's the difference between a greedy person and an electric toaster?

One takes the most and the other makes the toast

BOOK TITLES

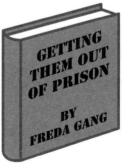

Chat challenge

What makes a good joke?
Is a good joke always about 'playing' with the meaning and sound of words?
Which jokes here depend upon the sound of words?
Which jokes depend upon a confusion over the meaning of words?

Comprehension

1) Which jokes depend upon 'puns' (a play on words)?

2) Which jokes depend upon clever use of the sound of words?

3) Why do the jokes containing the words **red** and **storeys** not really work when they are written down?

4) Which words do the writers expect you to know in these examples to get the clever joke?

5) How does the joke about the toaster and the greedy person work?

6) Why are the book titles and authors funny?

Objective focus

1) The following pairs of words are pronounced in the same way but they have different meanings. Write one sentence for each of the words.
   a. bear   bare   **c.** pear   pair
   b. piece   peace   **d.** cell   sell

2) Each of these words can mean two things. Write two sentences for each to show the different meanings.
   a. spring   **c.** seal
   b. train   **d.** ring

3) Complete the following so that they become jokes.
   a. I wondered why the football was getting bigger. Then it _____ me.

   b. I couldn't quite remember how to throw a boomerang, but eventually it came _____ to me.

   c. Did you hear about the guy whose whole left side was cut off? He's all _____ now.

Links to writing

1) Write some 'Knock, knock' jokes. Explain how they work. Use a computer to illustrate them and use speech bubbles. You could make a joke book.

2) Use puns (words that are similar and are used wrongly for a joke) to make up some more funny book titles and authors. You could stick them up around the class.

3) Imagine that you had to explain the jokes on the opposite page to someone who did not speak English very well. How would you do this?

Assess your
understanding   OK   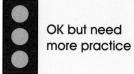 OK but need
more practice    not at all clear
and need to
revisit

17 What have we learned?

We've learned how to **understand and interpret texts**.

1 How and why we make notes to explain things

- Notes should highlight the most important bits of information.

- The most important bits might be key words, chunks of text, parts of a diagram or drawing.

- We have to be able to read notes but it's okay if they are written like this.

  They are not written in our best handwriting.

  They are bullet points.

  They are captions, labels, diagrams or drawings.

  They are highlighted or bracketed bits marked up in a text.

- Ask **Who? What? Where? When? Why? How?** to check that you have found the most important bits.

Check understanding!

 Make some notes on making notes – drawn or written – but make sure it works
for you.

2 How to understand the writer's perspective

- Writers can tell us what **they** think about a situation or character.

- Writers can tell us what they think by showing us what a **character** does or says.

- Writers can give us clues and imply what they think.

Check understanding!

 Write a piece about 'a boy you see in a railway station playing a guitar for money'.
What can you tell us about the boy and the situation?
Show us what the boy does or says.
**What details or clues can you give us about the boy? What do you want us to
understand about him?**

Assess your understanding

 OK

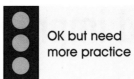 OK but need more practice

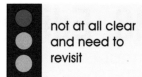 not at all clear and need to revisit

3 How to structure narrative texts

- It's essential to have a clear beginning, middle and end.

  Don't have too much going on for too long – but do have some action.

  Don't have too many characters and don't let them talk too much.

- A good beginning is really important.

  Start with an amazing piece of action.

  Start with a character saying something interesting.

  Hold back on the best bits – make the reader want to read on ...

- Plan a strong ending.

  Know your ending before you begin – don't just let it happen.

Check understanding!

Find a good story beginning (your own or in a book) and change it.

Find a good story ending (your own or in a book) and change it.

4 How to structure information texts

- We have looked at these text types:

  news reports   **instructions**   **non-chronological reports**   **formal letters**

Check understanding!

Choose a topic that interests you such as downloading music. Make notes as if you are going to write about it as a report, an instruction, a non-chronological report and a formal letter. You could use a chart to do this, e.g.

Downloading music Notes	News report	Instructions	Non-chronological report	Formal letter

5 How to use language to make people laugh

- A good joke plays with the meaning or sound of words.

Check understanding!

 Write out your favourite joke – explain to an alien why it is funny. What would make it even funnier?

18 Edit and improve your work

Little Wolf's Haunted Hall for Small Horrors

In this story, scary wolves are opening a scary new school.
Here is Little Wolf's letter home:

Dear Mum and Dad,

Please please PLEEEEZ don't be so grrrish. It's not fair Dad keeps saying, 'GET A MOVE ON LAZYBONES, OPEN YOUR SCHOOL QUICK.' Just because he has fang ache, I bet, boo shame. Today I will do news 1st, then cheery pics for him after.

Yeller and me and Stubbs are trying. Paws crossed we open soonly. But did you forget our 1 big problem I told you about before? I will tell you wunce more. It is the ghost of Uncle Bigbad. He is fine, in a dead way, but he keeps being orkwood nasty, saying do this and do that or no more haunting from me. Just because he knows we needed him for our School Spirit.

Ian Whybrow

Comprehension

1) Why do you think Little Wolf was writing this letter?

2) What appears to be the problem at the school?

3) Which words give you a clue that the writer is not a person?

4) Which words do you not recognise?

5) Can you guess what they mean?

6) Why do you think some words are written in capital letters?

Objective focus

1) Write the following in correct English and explain what you think is incorrect.

   a. I'll learn you.

   b. You was the first.

   c. I don't know nothing.

   d. The book what I read.

   e. He done it.

2) Rewrite the following phrases correctly and explain what you think is incorrect.

   a. She give me

   b. the actors was

   c. My mum don't let us

   d. I never saw nobody.

   e. Tracey done her work.

3) **Just because he has fang ache, I bet, boo shame**.
   Improve this sentence and write it correctly.

4) Which words in the passage opposite are not correctly spelled? Write them correctly. You may need to check in a dictionary.

Links to writing

1) Rewrite the passage in correct English. How does this change the impression we get of Little Wolf?

2) Continue the story of how they deal with Uncle Bigbad to get the school opened. What adventures would they have?

3) What might be on the timetable in this school for 'small horrors'? Design one.

4) Imagine that you have to tell a friend who is new to the school what it is really like, and the kind of things you get up to there. Write a letter containing this information.

19 Adapt non-narrative forms and styles

Here is some information about how to care for a kitten and a poem written about one.

A

- It's a good idea to prepare a place for your kitten: somewhere reasonably quiet, free of dangers (such as open windows), and clear of valuables. As you will discover, kittens and breakable objects tend to find each other fast!
- Let your kitten explore his new surroundings at his own pace. He will probably sleep a lot – up to 20 hours a day is normal (even adult cats sleep an average of 16 hours a day).
- If your kitten won't bed down in the place you have prepared for him, it's usually easiest to let him have his own way – by moving the bed and the kitten. Remember to place his feeding bowl, water and litter tray within easy reach.
- Once your kitten has settled in, he'll start to enjoy the affection you show him, so pick him up and talk to him.

B

Kitten

He arrived, frightened and loud, missing his mother and lost in a big, big new world.

He sits now, snuggled in the palm of my hand, purring, as I whisper to him.

He sleeps most of the time, curled around his tail, his nose tucked away.

He bats around a key on the floor, as if he were a footballer.

He hides behind the lid of his own cardboard-box bed, and jumps
out when I come near.

He investigates the outside world by leaning dangerously out of the window.

He runs around madly, bumping into anything, his fur spiky and his ears
tall like a bat's, and then he collapses and sleeps again.

He touches my ear with his wet nose when he sits on
my shoulder, his whole body vibrating.

He is a part of our family.

Chat challenge

Where do you think the first passage was printed? What is its purpose?
How is the purpose different from the poem's purpose?
Look at how both passages are set out. What do you notice?
Are these features important to the way they give information?
Which details can you find in both passages?

Comprehension

1) What danger to kittens does the writer highlight?

2) Why does the author suggest that you keep valuable items away from kittens?

3) How long do kittens sleep in the day? Do you find this surprising?

4) In the poem, how does the kitten feel when he arrives?

5) How do you know that the kitten is very small?

6) Why do you think the kitten's body vibrates?

7) What pattern do you notice the writer using in the poem?

Objective focus

1) Why do you think the writer uses bullet points in passage A?

2) Write some advice to a new pupil at your school about how to deal with the first day. Make notes first; then write sentences from them. Try using bullet points. Which is the easiest version to read? Using a computer to do this will be easier.

3) Read the passage on kittens in a different order. Does this make a difference to making sense of it? Why not?

4) In poems, you need to think about interesting descriptive words – the kitten does not **hit** the key – he **bats** it. Think of more descriptive verbs for the following.
   a. he said
   b. they walked
   c. she drank
   d. we ran

Links to writing

1) To write a poem using information, you will have to use your five senses. For each piece of information you use, think about touch, sight, smell, taste and hearing. Choose a piece of text from a history book, perhaps about a famous person.

2) Make notes of the most important facts. Think about comparisons – use **like** or **as**. What are these things like, e.g. **as if he were a footballer**?

3) Poems are easy when you use a pattern. In this poem each line starts with **He … .** You could use, **My hero …** or use a new characteristic for each line, e.g. **kindness is …**, **sadness is …**, etc. They do not have to rhyme. Type your pattern into a computer. Write, edit and publish your poem.

20 Viewpoint through the use of direct speech

Annie's Game

Annie was talking to someone who wasn't there.

Jack looked across the school playground at his sister. She was nodding her head and smiling at the empty space next to her, waving her hands around as she talked. Jack wondered briefly why he wasn't surprised. Nothing Annie did ought to surprise him any more. She was capable of anything, including having a conversation with thin air. Not that he cared what Annie was up to.

'Annie!' he called. 'Go and sit on the wall.'

Annie gave him a big smile.

'Can Sarah come with me?'

'What?' Jack turned to his sister.

'I said, "Can Sarah come with me?"'

'Sarah who?'

'Sarah Slade.' Annie pointed at the empty space next to her, a pleased look on her face.

'This is Sarah. She's my new friend. Say hello to Sarah, Jack.'

'There's no-one there,' Jack muttered.

'Yes there is,' Annie retorted, unruffled. 'She's just invisible, that's all.'

'Of course she is,' said Jack. 'Silly me. I should have realised.'

'Don't be sarcastic, Jack.' Annie opened her eyes wide, and gave him a superior stare. 'Sarah's a time-traveller you know. She's come to visit me from the future.'

Jack resisted a desire to bang his head against the nearest brick wall. It was a feeling he often had when he was alone with Annie.

Narinder Dhami

Chat challenge

Who is speaking here? How do you know?
Do you always need to tell your reader who is speaking?
Why is special punctuation necessary to show speech?
Are there any special features of how speech is set out?
How is this different from when you look at a playscript?

Comprehension

1) Where does the scene take place?

2) What is the relationship between Annie and Jack? Find the words that tell you.

3) What do you think is strange about Annie's behaviour?

4) What can Jack see her doing?

5) How does her brother react at first?

6) Who is Annie with?

7) What information do we learn about her **friend**?

8) What does **sarcastic** mean? You may need to look in a dictionary.

Objective focus

1) List any features you notice about how to punctuate speech, e.g. setting it out, position of punctuation.

2) Some words (adverbs) tell us the tone of voice of the speaker, e.g. **the man said indignantly**, **he replied impatiently**. Rewrite five speech sentences from the passage and include adverbs to show how Annie or Jack felt.

3) List any actions in the passage that show us how the characters feel about the situation.

Links to writing

1) The words people use tell us about how they feel. The way that the author reports those words also tells us about characters. Continue with the story opposite using some speech. Give us information as well, as the author would. How does Jack react? What is the reason for Annie's behaviour?

2) Speech creates a sense of character. Imagine someone in your class behaves like Annie, but her story turns out to be true. Write the story, which should include some speech. Show why you don't believe her at first. What has to happen before you know it's true? How do you feel then? If you use a computer program, it will be easier to put new speakers on new lines.

21 Viewpoint through the use of action

From Animorphs 1, The Invasion

Jake has changed into a lizard. This is what the world is like from his point of view.

I tried to think. Come on Jake. You have eyes on the side of your head now. They don't focus together. They see different things. Deal with it.

I tried to make sense of the pictures, using this knowledge, but they were still a mess. It seems to take me forever to figure it out. One eye was looking down the hall to the left. The other was looking down the hall on the right. I was upside down, gripping the side of the locker, which was like a long, grey field that wouldn't end.

Suddenly I was off and running. Straight down the wall. Zoom! Then on level floor. Zoom! The ground flew past. It was like being strapped on to a crazy, out-of-control missile.

Then my lizard brain sensed the spider. It was a strange thing, like I wasn't sure if I saw the spider, or heard it, or smelled it, or tasted it on my flicking lizard tongue, or just suddenly knew that it was there.

I took off after it, racing at a million miles an hour before I could think about stopping. My legs were a blur, they moved so fast.

The spider ran. I ran after it. I was faster.

Noooooooo! I screamed inside my head.

K A Applegate

Chat challenge

What sort of book does this passage come from?
What makes it exciting? Do you want to know what happens next?
Do you think it relies on action for its excitement? Why? It's not really about action.
Imagine a story without action – what would it be like?
If a story was all action, would it work? Why not?

Comprehension

1) What is the first thing that Jake notices?

2) What does he find strange about this?

3) What does the locker remind him of? Why should this be?

4) When he runs, which words tell you that he is travelling fast?

5) What does he compare his speed to?

6) Why does he race after the spider?

Objective focus

1) To describe action, you need to use **action verbs**. Describe how you would do the following actions and explain the differences between them.

    a. flick the pages of a book   **c.** wring your hands

    b. knead dough   **d.** drum your fingers

2) Use these verbs and write sentences to describe how an old person might try to find a ticket in her bag.

    a. fumble   **b.** grope   **c.** twiddle

    Add two expressive verbs of your own.

3) Describe (or even act out) the differences between the following.

    a. lounge and sit   **c.** write and scribble   **e.** look and peer

    b. trudge and walk   **d.** throw and hurl   **f.** poke and nudge

Links to writing

1) What happens at the end of the story? Continue with it using the same point of view. You will need to think about the characteristics of a lizard. What might it see, hear, feel?

2) Imagine that you have been changed into a different animal, e.g. a cat. What would the world be like from your point of view? What adventures would you have?

Research on the Internet to find out some characteristics of the animal.

Think about onomatopoeic words (**zoom!**) you could use to describe your actions.

Use strong verbs to describe your actions.

Use all your senses: how would they change in your new situation?

22 Viewpoint through the use of detail

THE OTTERBURY INCIDENT

Johnny Sharp wore a grey homburg hat, rather on the back of his head and cocked sideways, with the brim turned down in front. He had a foxy sort of face – narrow eyes, long thin nose, long thin lips; he grinned a lot, allowing his bad teeth and gold-stopped one on the left of his upper jaw to show. He had a loud checked suit with padded shoulders, and a perfectly ghastly tie with large patterns on it like drawing-room curtains. He had two flashy rings on his right hand, and a habit of flopping his hand at you while he was talking. He was a narrow, wriggling sort of a chap, from top to bottom; like a dressed-up eel.

Or a snake.

C Day Lewis

Chat challenge

When you are describing someone, why is detail necessary?

What are adjectives?

What are adverbs?

Why are they useful in sentences?

Do you like this person?

Do you think the author wants you to like him? Why?

Comprehension

1) List the features that the author chooses to describe, e.g. hat, face, etc.

2) What details does the author choose to give about those features?

3) What kind of adjectives does he use to describe shape, size, colour, etc.?

4) He also describes the character's mannerisms. Find some examples.

5) Which words tell you that the author does not like Johnny?

6) Which comparisons tell you this as well?

7) What makes you not like this character?

Objective focus

1) Choose ten nouns from things around you on the desk. Now choose four adjectives to describe their shape, size, colour and texture.

2) Write a description for the police of someone in you class who is lost. This should concentrate on the facts only. What features will you choose?
How will you know that the details you have chosen are factual only?

3) Write the same description as if you did not like this person. Which adjectives will you use to show your feelings?

4) Choose someone you know to write a description. List the features you want to describe, e.g. hair. Ask yourself questions about this to gather detail, e.g. What did it look like before?

Links to writing

1) Add adjectives to each noun in the following sentence to make the longest, most detailed sentence you can.
'I want a tent, please,' said the boy to the man in the sports shop.

2) Now edit the very long sentence in Question 1 to make it shorter but more effective. Prove that a long sentence is not always best. (Using a computer will make editing easier.)

3) Now develop this sentence into a story. Use descriptions to make the story more interesting. When you are writing, remember to ask yourself Where? When? How? The answers will give you interesting ideas.

Assess your
understanding

 OK

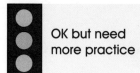 OK but need
more practice

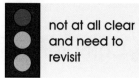 not at all clear
and need to
revisit

23 What have we learned?

We've learned how to **create and shape texts**.

1 How to edit and improve work

- Look at the draft and check the following.

  the genres or text type

  the original purpose

  whether it meets the needs of the audience

  the content

  the layout – how does it look?

  spelling and grammar

Check understanding!

 Check a piece of your own recent work and review and edit it using the
bullets above.

2 How to adapt non-narrative forms and styles

- Assess the style of the writing you are going to change. What text type is it?

- Check it. Look for clues about audience, vocabulary, layout, organisation, grammar
  and punctuation, plus any other features that you notice. What features are always
  the same?

- What new features will you need to change it from one to the other?

Check understanding!

 Select a piece of non-narrative writing from a leaflet or book. Make a spider
diagram of the new features you will need to change it into a poem, a story and a
different sort of factual text.

3 How to explore viewpoint through speech

- Speech marks show when a character is speaking and what they are actually saying.

- When a character starts to speak, use a new paragraph and a capital letter inside
  the speech mark.

Assess your
understanding  OK   OK but need
more practice   not at all clear
and need to
revisit

Check understanding!

Write out this text using direct speech features and avoiding the use of **said**.

I wasn't running away. Not proper running away. Not really, Jason said inside his head as he stood at the edge of the platform with his bag in his hand.

4 How to explore viewpoint through action

- Speech can tell us what a character is doing and why.

  'I can't hang on!' she sobbed, as she swung precariously from side to side over the precipice.

- Using powerful action verbs can also help us to understand a viewpoint; what the character is doing, how it's being done and why.

  He swam away. → He lashed out with his arms and legs in the water as he fought to escape the clutches of the gyrating tentacles of this monstrous beast.

- Remember that adverbs tell us how an action is being done: **He ate. → He ate voraciously.** Try hard to use unusual vocabulary to create interest.

Check understanding!

Find three sentences in your reading book that explore a character's viewpoint through action. Identify the verbs and explain how they make a difference.

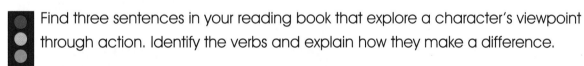

5 How to explore viewpoint through detail

- To describe things well, use interesting vocabulary – nouns, adjectives and adverbs.

- Describe the characters in a story and what is happening, in a way that helps the reader to understand the characters better. Describe their feelings and moods but also try to bring across how you as a writer feel about them.

Check understanding!

Describe a character so that it is obvious that you don't like them and then describe a character so that it is obvious that you really admire them.

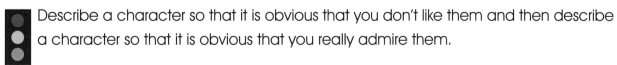

24 Paragraphs and order

Money

Before money was invented people had to buy and sell by exchanging things. A farmer might exchange his surplus wheat for a horse or a cow that one of his neighbours did not need; but first he had to find another farmer who wanted wheat and who had a horse or cow to spare.

Even after money was invented, it was not always the convenient shape that it is today. In the past many things have been used for money – blocks of salt, shells and beads.

Eventually people realised that metal was the most suitable substance to make money from. It was valuable, did not wear out and could be made into convenient sizes. Gold, silver and copper were the three metals most commonly used. The value of the coin was the value of the amount of gold, silver or copper that it contained, so every time business took place the coins had to be weighed.

The next stage was to make coins in a much wider range of weights. These weights and a symbol of the country were stamped on the coins.

Today coins are valuable, but not because they are made of valuable metals; there are no gold coins made today. Coins and paper money have value because a government has agreed that each note or coin shall be worth its face value, which is the amount stamped on it.

Chat challenge

Why is it important to write in paragraphs?
If this passage was not written in paragraphs, would it be as easy to read?
How do we know when to end one paragraph and start another?
What is each of these five paragraphs about?
If you were to change the order of the paragraphs here, would it make a difference?

Comprehension

1) What did people do before money was invented?

2) What was the problem with this system?

3) What strange things have been used as a form of money?

4) What kinds of metal has money been made out of?

5) Why was the weight of a coin important?

6) How do we know the value of present-day coins?

Objective focus

1) Identify the sentence (topic sentence) that tells you what each paragraph will be about. Write it at the centre of a spider diagram and write notes around it, using the detail in each paragraph.

2) Look at the words that begin each paragraph. Identify clues that tell you the paragraphs are in the right time order.

3) Read the paragraphs in a different order. Does the passage make sense now? Why not?

4) Write five paragraphs about the history of something else, e.g. toys, computers, football. (You may need to do some research on your topic.) Use the following words to start your paragraphs.
   before   eventually   the next stage   today

Links to writing

1) Describe in three paragraphs the place where you live. Use the following plan.
   a. In the first paragraph, describe the whole area and its features.
   b. In the second paragraph, describe one part of this area.
   c. In the third paragraph, describe one small thing in this part.
   In this way, you are acting like a camera, zooming in on something.

2) Check that you are using paragraphs correctly, that you have a topic sentence and that when you talk about something new, you start a new paragraph.

25 Changing the order of sentences

Surnames

Did you ever wonder where the word 'surname' comes from? The prefix *sur-* means 'over and above' or 'additional to', and surnames are additional names, or names added to a child's personal name. A child's surname was not always the same as his or her father's; in the Middle Ages surnames were a kind of nickname and might have come from the work that a person did or from where they lived.

Perhaps the commonest surnames are occupational names. In the past, a Smith was a man who smited or worked in metal, so today we have names such as Goldsmith – a man who smited in gold. A Wright was a man who worked with wood; a Mason worked in stone, and the origin of names such as Taylor and Thatcher are obvious.

Surnames that were the names of natural features in the country also became common. Before there were addresses in the countryside there might have been two Richards in the same area – one living near a wood and one near a field. So they became Richard Woods and Richard Field to distinguish them.

Chat challenge

Why is it important to write in paragraphs?
If this passage was not written in paragraphs, would it be easy to read?
How do we know when to end one paragraph and start another?
Which sentence tells you what each of these paragraphs is really about?
What does the rest of the paragraph add to this?

Comprehension

1) Why were people given surnames? In which paragraph did you find the information?

2) Where does **surname** come from? In which paragraph did you find the information?

3) Mention two ways in which surnames were formed. In which paragraph did you find the information?

4) Using the information in the passage, decide which one is the odd one out in each group and say why.

   a. Mason   Johnson   Painter   Tyler   **c.** Moore   Dale   Hill   Smith

   b. Goldsmith   Baxter   Brook

Objective focus

1) The following paragraph needs to be broken up into sentences.

Every other Monday I go to my Club but we are moving soon to a new house and I think I will have to stop going because of the journey which would be pleasant in summer but not good in winter when the nights are cold and dark especially if you like sitting in front of the TV like me.

2) Paragraph 1 contains three sentences. Number them 1, 2 and 3. Rewrite them in a different order, e.g. what happens to the sense of the paragraph if you write them in the order of 2, 1, 3 or 2, 3, 1? Why does the writer start the paragraph with the question? What do the other sentences do?

3) Try this with the other two paragraphs. What happens to the sense? What conclusions can you draw about the order of sentences?

Links to writing

1) Write the topic sentences in the three paragraphs on the opposite page. List under them, in note form, the more detailed information given. You could do this as a spider diagram.

2) Suppose a fourth topic sentence was: In modern times, other cultures have settled in Britain and brought in new names. Give some detail to illustrate this.

3) Use the following two sets of sentences as topic sentences. Write more about each paragraph but write notes to start with. (You could do this on a computer so that it will be easier to rewrite your notes as sentences. You may need to do some research.)

   a. It is hot in Africa during the day. The nights are often cold.

   b. Venice is a famous city. It is in Italy. It has canals and no streets.

26 Speech marks

The Adventures of Tom Sawyer

About noon the next day the boys arrived at the dead tree; they had come for their tools. Tom was impatient to go to the haunted house. Huck Finn suddenly said …

'Looky here Tom, do you know what day it is?'

Tom ran mentally over the days of the week and then quickly lifted his eyes with a startled look in them.

'My! I never once thought of it, Huck.'

'Well, I didn't neither, but all at once it popped on me that it was Friday.'

'Blame it; a body can't be too careful, Huck. We might 'a' got into an awful scrape, tackling such things on a Friday.'

'*Might*! Better say we *would*! There's some lucky days, maybe, but Friday ain't.'

'Any fool knows that. I don't reckon YOU was the first that found it out, Huck.'

'Well, I never said I was, did I? And Friday ain't all, neither. I had a rotten dream last night … dreamt about rats.'

'No! Sure sign of trouble. Did they fight?'

'No.'

'Well, that's good, Huck. When they don't fight, it's only a sign that there's trouble around, you know. All we got to do is look mighty sharp and keep out of it. We'll drop this thing for today, and play. Do you know Robin Hood, Huck?'

'No. Who's Robin Hood?'

'Why he was one of the greatest men that ever lived in England … and the best. … We'll play Robin Hood … it's nobby fun. I'll learn you.'

'I'm agreed.'

So they played Robin Hood all the afternoon, now and then casting a yearning eye down upon the haunted house.

Mark Twain

Comprehension

1) Name the two characters speaking in the passage.

2) Why have they met by the dead tree?

3) What stops them going to the house?

4) What is their view of Friday?

5) Do you find this strange? Why?

6) What else happened to make them concerned?

7) How do you know who is speaking each time?

 ## Objective focus

1) List any features you notice about how to punctuate speech, e.g. setting it out, position of punctuation.

2) Punctuate this passage correctly.

Look out warned the passenger

Whats the matter muttered the driver half asleep

Sorry the passenger answered apologetically I thought you were going to crash

3) We can use verbs other than **said** to tell us how the speaker felt, e.g. he growled, the man shouted, he pleaded. Use the following in some speech sentences rather than **said**.

a. yelled   **c.** sobbed   **e.** roared

b. murmured   **d.** whispered

 ## Links to writing

1) In speech you can use non-standard English. Find examples of this in the passage. Write them out correctly. What difference does it make to your view of the character?

2) Imagine that Huck and Tom come back the next day to visit the house. Write about what happens. Use speech, employing the features of speech that you noticed.

3) Word process a set of rules for the punctuation of speech that can be displayed in your classroom. Find images that you can use which will make the rules attractive and mean that others understand them better.

27 Apostrophes

King Arthur

King Arthur was dying. He'd lost the great battle and many of his knights were dead. Only Launcelot's friends, brave Sir Lucan and Sir Bedivere were left.

Camelot's castles were visible in the mist, as the two knights carried the King's body to his last resting place. They found a little deserted chapel. The King's voice was faint and he sighed as he looked up at the last Knights of the Round Table.

'We're all that's left,' he said. 'Don't feel sad. There is one final duty that you, Sir Bedivere, must perform for me.'

'Anything, my King,' said the Knight. 'I'm here to serve you.'

'My time's short. Take my sword Excalibur which I pulled from the stone when I was a boy. It must be returned to the Lady of the Lake. Walk yonder a mile from here and you'll find a large lake. Throw the sword into the water. Return and tell me what you see.' The king turned in pain as he produced the magnificent Excalibur. It was the most powerful sword in the world, and had magical powers. Its hilt was covered in precious stones.

Sir Bedivere said, 'My Lord. You're my King,' and lifting the sword delicately in his hands, he walked away over the mountains.

He found the lake as the King had said but just as he was about to throw the sword into the dark waters, he heard a voice in his ear.

'Don't throw this power away. It could be all yours. How will the King know? He's almost dead.'

Sir Bedivere thought for a while and the voice's power took over his mind. He betrayed his King and broke his knight's vows. He hid the sword in a bush and returned to the King.

'What did you see my brave knight?' asked Arthur, struggling to raise himself from the ground.

'Nothing, my liege, but the water's ripple as I threw in the sword.'

'Liar and traitor! You have betrayed all knights' trust!' screamed the King.

He knew that the Lady of the Lake's bargain was to reclaim her gift to him.

Chat challenge

Why do writers use apostrophes?
Are they really useful in sentences?
Do apostrophes always come before an *s*?
What would happen if you removed the apostrophes – would it make a difference to your understanding of the passage?
What problems would this cause?

Comprehension

1) Name the only two knights left.

2) Where did they take King Arthur? Why?

3) What does he ask Sir Bedivere to do?

4) What happens when he tries to do it?

5) What does he tell King Arthur?

6) How does the King react?

Objective focus

1) Identify where apostrophes are used in the passage. Sort the examples into two columns: for **Showing possession** and **Letters left out**.

2) Write out the shortened forms of the following words with their apostrophes.

   a. cannot   **c.** what has   **e.** they have

   b. it is   **d.** I have   **f.** they are

3) Match up the words in the two columns. You will first have to use the words **of the** and then put in an apostrophe, e.g. the frame of the picture – the picture's frame.

   a. the frame   dresses

   b. a dog   anchors

   c. two ships   book

   d. the ladies   picture

   e. the author   paintings

   f. many artists   collar

Links to writing

1) Put the apostrophes in two different places in these examples and explain the difference in meaning.

   a. the cats kittens   **c.** the girls dresses

   b. my brothers books   **d.** the farmers fields

2) You have to teach other children in the class about apostrophes. Create a character **Super Apostrophe** to make things fun. Write his adventures with words. Remember – you have to tell people where, how and why to use apostrophes.

Assess your understanding OK

 OK but need more practice

 not at all clear and need to revisit

28 What have we learned?

We've learned about **text structure and organisation**.

1 How to order paragraphs for different effects

- Paragraphs are groups of sentences that are all about the same topic or person.

- Start a new paragraph each time something new happens or when you give a new piece of information.

- Paragraphs help us to break up our work into meaningful units but you can change the order of the units for a different effect.

Check understanding!

 Write out five starters for five paragraphs from a story book. Could they be reordered?

2 How to order sentences within paragraphs for different effects

- The topic sentence is a sentence that sets out the main idea or topic of a paragraph.

> **Make sure you know what your main idea is!**

- It is often the first sentence, especially when arguing a point, where it may well be followed by further information, examples, etc.

- Use a range of connectives to join sentences in different ways and to make your sentences different lengths.

Check understanding!

 Select a non-fiction paragraph and identify the topic sentence and the sentences that follow, saying what each does. Try to re-order them to create a different effect.

Assess your understanding OK  OK but need more practice  not at all clear and need to revisit

We've learned about **sentence structure and punctuation**.

3 How to use speech marks

- Speech marks show when a character is speaking and what they are actually saying when we quote them.

- When a character starts to speak, use a new paragraph and a capital letter inside the speech mark.

- Note that there is a comma **before** the speech starts, and a full stop at the end but **inside** the speech marks, if it is the end of the sentence.
  John said, 'This is easy.'

- Note that there is punctuation **inside** the closing speech marks, if the sentence continues after the speech.

Check understanding!

 Find five examples of direct speech from books or your own writing and make the following changes.
Change the verb (e.g. 'said' to 'reported').
Change the position of the bit of the sentence that tells us who is talking, and the punctuation to match (e.g. John said → said John).

4 How to use apostrophes

- Apostrophes are used to show us that something belongs to a person or a number of people.
  The King's voice was faint – in other words the voice belongs to the King.
  The Kings' orders were loud – in other words there are two Kings giving orders.

  Its, **his** and **hers** don't need an apostrophe even though they are showing us that something belongs to someone.

- Apostrophes are also used to indicate missing letters.
  Can't is the same as cannot.
  It's means it is or it has.

> **Never use an apostrophe for a plural**

Check understanding!

 Write ten quiz questions on apostrophes for your friends to answer – be really mean and include some exceptions to challenge them (but make sure you also write out the answer sheet!).

Glossary

adjective   a word that comes before a noun and gives us more detail about it

adverb   a word that comes after a verb and gives us detail about the action of the verb

apostrophe   a punctuation mark (') used to indicate either possession or the omission of letters or numbers

consonants   all letters except a, e, i, o, u

derivation   where something has come from

joke   words that make people laugh through the use of sound or meaning

mnemonic   anything that helps us to remember something else

narrative   the recounting or telling of past events: account, chronicle, description, list, story, report, statement

onomatopoeia   a word that sounds like its meaning

paragraph   groups of sentences that are all about the same topic, separated from the rest of the text by a line space above and below it or by indenting the first line (leaving a space between the margin and the first word). A paragraph usually contains sentences that deal with one topic, and a new paragraph signals a change of topic.

perspective   someone's viewpoint or opinion

plural   means more than one of something

prefix   a letter pattern fixed to the beginning of a word which affects its meaning

punctuation   the symbols used in written language to indicate the end of a sentence or a clause, or to indicate that it is a question, etc. The punctuation symbols most commonly used in English are **. , ; : ' ? ! " – " " ( ).**

reported speech   what someone else said, but without using the exact words, e.g. 'I'm going to come.' → He said that he was going to come.

singular   means one of something

speech marks   punctuation marks that show us when a character is speaking

suffix   a letter pattern fixed to the end of a word which affects its meaning

topic sentence   a sentence that sets out the main idea of a paragraph

unstressed vowels   vowels that are written but not pronounced clearly, or at all, in some words.

viewpoint   somebody's perspective or opinion

vocabulary   the words we use

vowels   a, e, i, o, u

A reminder of the literacy topics you will probably have been studying in Y5

Narrative plays and scripts	novels and stories by significant authors	traditional stories, fables, myths and legends	stories from other cultures	older literature	film narratives	dramatic conventions
Non-fiction	instructions		recounts		persuasive writing	
Poetry	poetic style: word-play, rhyme, metaphor, word choice		classic/narrative poems		choral and performance	

Handy hints

Ten tips on handwriting

1 Keep the letters simple – no exaggerated flicks and curls.

2 Keep the letters on the line – no wandering up or down!

3 Keep the letter the same size – no huge letters appearing suddenly in the middle of a word.

4 Keep it well-spaced – no huge gaps in the hope that you will have to write less, and no squashed sentences are hard to read.

5 Keep your capital letters and lower case letters looking different; even when they look the same, e.g. for *s*, the capital must be bigger than the lower case.

6 Keep the small letters the same height and the tall letters the same height (apart from *t* which is a bit shorter than the others).

7 Letters which are tall or have tails don't need to be **very** tall or have **very** long tails; keep them under control.

8 Letters which are tall or have tails need to be straight or slanting **in the same direction**.

9 If you make a mistake then deal with it just **once**: rub it out, or put one line through it, or put it in brackets. Write the correct word clearly above it or at the side and move on.

10 If **you** can't read it then chances are that no one else can either. Keep it neat all the time.

Rules for capital letters

people's names

people's titles (like **Mrs** Jones)

places

days of the week

months of the year

organisations

Full stops

Always put a full stop at the end of a sentence, unless you are using a **?** or a **!**

Spelling

Ten tips on spelling

1 Say the word in your head and listen to it.

2 Write it down and look at it. Does it look right? If not, what changes would make sense?

3 Spelling is either right or wrong (no grey areas) so choose carefully.

4 If it's a long word – don't panic. **Say it, listen to it, write it down or just the bits you know.**

5 Most long words are made up of smaller words or chunks of letters.

6 Some long words have little words inside them – look out for them. There's a 'rat' in **separate** – make them up yourself!

7 Get to know your sound choices – if it's an *n* sound that you hear at the beginning of a word, then know that the choices are *n*, *kn* or even *gn* (as in **gnat**)!

8 Get to know some basics – lots of words have bits stuck on the front (prefixes) and lots have bits stuck on the end (suffixes). Know them and use them.

9 Look for patterns – if it's **baby/babies** then it stands a good chance of being **city/cities**.

10 Get the easy ones right! No excuses for getting words wrong that you need to use all the time, like **the**, **said**, **tomorrow**.

If you find a word that breaks the rule or pattern, then **learn it fast** so that it doesn't catch you out next time.

OH! And don't always rely on the spell check when working on the computer – keep thinking for yourself so that when you are writing you don't get stuck.

OH! And don't spell the word right but then get the apostrophe wrong because that makes the whole thing wrong. Use the apostrophe to show you who owns what (**Ben's dinner**), for groups of people (**The Rising Stars' offices**) and to make two words into one (**I am → I'm**).

Rising Stars UK Ltd, 22 Grafton Street, London W1S 4EX

www.risingstars-uk.com

Acknowledgements

Unit 8 p18 – Extract from *The Runner* – Keith Gray published by Corgi Yearling. Reprinted by permission of the Random House Group Ltd.

Unit 9 p20 – Extract from *Buried Alive* by Jacqueline Wilson, published by Corgi Yearling. Reprinted by permission of the Random House Group Ltd.

Unit 10 p22 – Dennis the Menace cartoon, DC Thomson & Co. From *The Kingfisher BEANO File*, Rhymes and Riddles by Fran Pickering, Kingfisher, 1996

Unit 18 p38 – Extract from *Little Wolf's Haunted Hall for Small Horrors* by Ian Whybrow, Collins Children's Books. Reprinted by permission of Harper Collins Publishers. © Ian Whybrow 1999

Unit 20 p42 – Extract from *Annie's Game* by Narinder Dhami, published by Corgi Yearling. Reprinted by permission of the Random House Group Ltd.

Extract from The *Invasion (Animorphs 1)* by K. A. Applegate, 1996. Scholastic Paperbacks

Unit 22 p46 – Extract from *The Otterbury Incident* by C Day Lewis, published by The Bodley Head. Reprinted by permission of Random House Group

Every effort has been made to trace copyright holders and obtain their permission for the use of copyright materials. The authors and publisher will gladly receive information enabling them to rectify any error or omission in subsequent editions.

All facts are correct at time of going to press.

Published 2007

Text, design and layout © Rising Stars UK Ltd.

Design: HL Studios

Illustrations: HL Studios

Editorial project management: Dodi Beardshaw

Editorial: Dodi Beardshaw

Cover design: Burville-Riley Design

British Library Cataloguing in Publication Data.

A CIP record for this book is available from the British Library.

ISBN: 978-1-84680-095-5

Printed by: Gutenberg Press, Malta